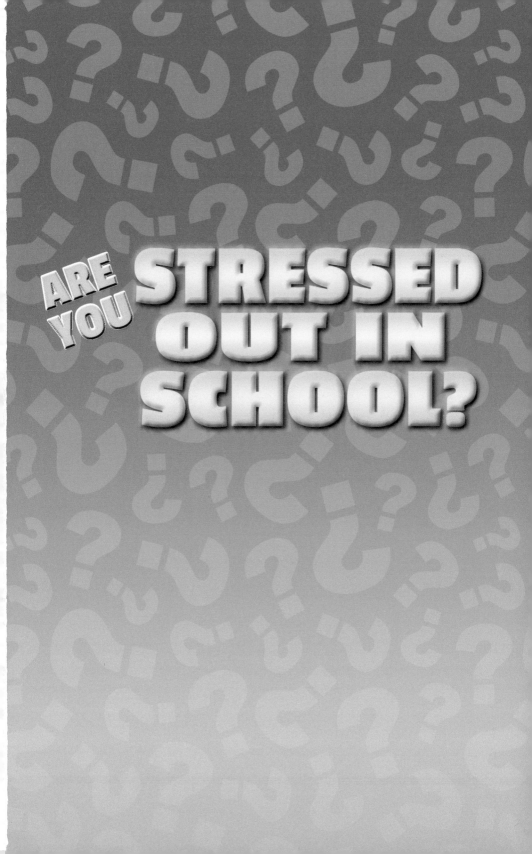

ARE YOU STRESSED OUT IN SCHOOL?

Stephanie
Sammartino
McPherson

TESTING

PEERPRESSURE

SCHEDULING

GRADUATING

LACK OF SLEEP

EXPECTATIONS

Enslow Publishing
101 W. 23rd Street
Suite 240
New York, NY 10011
USA

enslow.com

In loving memory of four gifted teachers:
Marion Sammartino, whose humor and energy always inspired her students
Angelo Sammartino, who made history come alive
Marie McPherson, who made learning joyful for first graders
Lorraine Andrews, whose love of French and Spanish was infectious

Acknowledgments

I would like to thank the following people: Gayle Hamilton, Maria Edmunds, Jonathan Sammartino, Lana Krumweide, Tim Bedley, Paul Fleisher, Mickey VanDerwerker, Claudia Porter, Jeffrey Doyle, Bryan Carr, Sarah Mansfield, Autumn Nabors, and Jennifer Coleman, Elizabeth McGhee, and my husband, Richard McPherson.

Published in 2016 by Enslow Publishing, LLC
101 W. 23rd Street, Suite 240, New York, NY 10011

Cataloging-in-Publication Data

McPherson, Stephanie Sammartino.
  Are you stressed out in school? / by Stephanie Sammartino McPherson.
    p. cm. —(Got issues?)
  Includes bibliographical references and index.
  ISBN 978-0-7660-6983-1 (library binding)
  1. Students — Mental health — United States — Juvenile literature. 2. Stress management — United States —Juvenile literature. 3. Stress (Psychology) — Prevention — Juvenile literature. I. McPherson, Stephanie Sammartino. II. Title.
  LB3430.M38 2016
  371.713—d23

Printed in the United States of America

To Our Readers: We have done our best to make sure all Web site addresses in this book were active and appropriate when we went to press. However, the author and the publisher have no control over and assume no liability for the material available on those Web sites or on any Web sites they may link to. Any comments or suggestions can be sent by e-mail to customerservice@enslow.com.

Portions of this book originally appeared in the book *Stressed Out in School? Learning to Deal With Academic Pressure.*

Disclaimer: For many of the images in this book, the people photographed are models. The depictions do not imply actual situations or events.

Photo Credits: Andrey_Popov/Shutterstock.com, p. 89; Anelina/Shutterstock.com, p. 39; Amir Ridhwan/Shutterstock.com, p. 96; Amy Johansson/Shutterstock.com, p. 25; antoniodiaz/Shutterstock.com, p. 81; Basar/Shutterstock.com, p.51; Bronson Chang/Shutterstock.com, p. 63; Cherries/Shutterstock.com, p. 30; Courtesy of Marion Sammartino, p. 71; Feng Yu/Shutterstock.com, p. 7; FilmMagic/Getty Images, p. 91; Hailshadow/iStock/Thinkstock, p. 64; HansKim/iStock/Thinkstock, p. 3; Intellistudies/Shutterstock.com, p. 56; Joshua Resnick/Shutterstock.com, p. 58; Kapnia Aliaksei,Shutterstock.com, p. 104; katarinag/Shutterstock.com, p. 45; Kim Reinick/Shutterstock.com, p. 33; Konstantin L./Shutterstock.com, pp. 61, 68; Lambert/Archive Photos/Getty Images, p. 36; Laurence Gough/Shutterstock.com, p. 67; Lisa F. Young/Shutterstock.com, p. 13; martiapunts/Shutterstock.com, p. 22; Michael C. Gray/Shutterstock.com, p. 35; Netfalls-Remy Musser/Shutterstock.com, p. 42; oliveromg/Shutterstock.com, p. 99; Paul Matthew Photography/Shutterstock.com, p. 9; Pavel L. Photo and Video/Shutterstock.com, p. 101; PETER CLOSE/Shutterstock.com, p. 73; Pressmaster/Shutterstock.com, p. 15; Piotr Marcinski/Shutterstock.com, p. 48; runzelkorn/Shutterstock.com, pp. 47, 86; Sabphoto/Shutterstock.com, p. 79; sebra/Shutterstock.com, p. 77; Tupungato/Shutterstock.com, p. 53; ubanbuzz/Shutterstock.com, p. 93; Volt Collection/Shutterstock.com, p. 17; VGstockstudio/Shutterstock.com, p. 84; Zou Zou/Shutterstock.com, p. 20.

Cover Credit: HansKim/iStock/Thinkstock (stressed teen).

Contents

An A for Everyone?

Maria Mitchell never went to college. She never studied educational psychology or worried about assessing academic progress. But if you asked her students, young women at Vassar College in the late 1800s, they would have told you she was a born teacher. Maria loved her subject matter, astronomy, and she loved being with young people. It was a win-win situation for everyone. Observation and hands-on experience were the hallmarks of Maria's teaching. Whenever a meteor shower occurred, she would run through the dorms to awaken her students and lead them to the rooftop of the college observatory.

There was only one thing Maria disliked about teaching—grades. She sometimes joked that if a student came to class well prepared, then that student deserved an A for achievement. If a student came to class partially prepared, the that student deserved an A for effort.

And if a student came to class totally unprepared, then that student deserved A for courage in daring to show up at all.[1]

Adventure or Source of Stress?

Maria Mitchell expected hard work from her students, and she got it. Almost all educators will tell you that this is the way it should be—students working hard for love of learning. But it does not always turn out this way. Instead of an adventure, school has become a source of stress to some students. They worry about their classroom performance and their class ranking. They fear that if they fall behind, they will not get into a good college. For such students, the subject matter becomes secondary to the grades they earn. The pressure they feel may actually make it harder for them to learn.

Of course, not all pressure is harmful. In fact, it is almost impossible to imagine a world without it. Adults face pressure to earn enough money, pressure to do their jobs well, and pressure to please family and friends. They have deadlines and responsibilities to meet. These demands can be good things as long as they do not become overwhelming.

The same thing is true of academic pressure. It is not all bad. For example, a Spanish test on Friday may be just the spur you need to learn those new vocabulary words. In a similar way, writing a history paper can give someone a chance to explore people and ideas in greater depth than in the classroom. Ideally, this should be something you enjoy doing.

The question is not how to free students from all pressure. It is how much pressure and what kind of assignments make for the best learning situations. What works well for one student may not necessarily work well for another. Yet teachers lack the time and resources to individualize assignments for every student. Like many of the children in their classrooms, they often feel anxious and overworked. Some educators and parents believe that much of the problem has to do with the growing demands placed on teachers by mandated standardized testing. Children are being asked to master

School can seem like a source of stress, but considering it an adventure can change your perspective. Instead of creating anxiety, you may find that school is an opportunity for exploration and improvement.

material at younger ages. In many instances, teachers are judged not so much on the quality of their instruction as on how well their students perform on standardized tests.

"Speeding Up the Assembly Line"

Child psychologist David Elkind captured the essence of the problem in the title of his groundbreaking book *The Hurried Child: Growing Up Too Fast Too Soon*. Elkind is concerned about the practice of cramming more subject matter into the earlier grades. He calls this an "assembly line" approach to education. "There is a tendency to speed up the assembly line," he writes, "to increase production. Why not put in as much at kindergarten as at first grade? Why not teach fourth grade math at grade two? Indeed, as

Polar Opposites

Students respond to academic pressure in many different ways. Some students are like Jonas Salk, the doctor who developed the first polio vaccine in the 1950s. A model student, Salk was well-organized, studied hard, and helped classmates with difficult material. He thrived under pressure and tough assignments.

Albert Einstein, his polar opposite in the classroom, found the strict routines of his schools boring and irritating. Although he got good grades, he was surly and disrespectful to his teachers. One even told Einstein that he would never amount to anything. Finally, his high school teachers had enough. They expelled the boy who would grow up to become one of the greatest scientists the world has ever known.

Students may come to school with a wide range of attitudes, aptitudes, and the ability to weather stress. They may be industrious and conscientious like Salk, rebellious and stubborn like Einstein, or anywhere in between. But everyone faces school pressure at some time or another. It's important to remember that you can control the pressure. It doesn't have to control you.

one professor mused, why not teach philosophy at grade three?"[2] Some observers might call Elkind's words a good description of the current educational scene. However, his book was published in 1981. Clearly the phenomenon of urging children to achieve more at younger ages has been around for a while.

Long before Elkind, noted European psychologist Jean Piaget also taught that intellectual growth cannot be rushed. Each child has his or her own inner schedule.[3] Some are ready to read early and others later. The slower developing child is not less capable than his or her more rapidly advancing classmates. His or her natural abilities are simply unfolding at a different rate. This is not a problem unless schools make it a problem.

Why are children being pushed so quickly in the twenty-first century? How did this acceleration begin? Does school pressure prepare students to face the demands of the adult world better? Does it help them get better jobs? Does it make them happier? Or would children do better with less stress and a more relaxed timetable to learning?

There are no easy answers to these questions. However, there are ways to combat stress and lead a balanced life despite homework, tests, and grades.

This book will take a look at the current education situation, how it got this way, and what you can do to alleviate stress in your own school life. Maria Mitchell's idea of an A for everyone may not be looming on the horizon. But pleasure in new ideas, growing self-confidence, and yes, a little bit of pressure (It's not all bad!) can go hand-in-hand in an optimum educational experience.

Grade School and Middle School: "So Little Time to Be Kids"

Children start to learn long before they enter grade school. Almost from the moment of birth, babies begin to take in their surroundings. Over the next weeks and months, they learn to recognize the faces and voices of their mothers, fathers, and siblings. They start to reach for objects then discover how to manipulate them. There is no difference for them between playing and learning. You may have observed this yourself as you watch a younger sibling fit triangles, circles, and squares into a shape sorter. Or play peek-a-boo by hiding behind a sofa cushion. Or energetically create masterpieces of colorful scribbles with jumbo crayons.

When they start preschool or kindergarten, children are like little sponges that are curious and ready to absorb all kinds of learning. Once again, play is crucial to their social and intellectual development. They learn to make friends, share, play by the rules of the game, and listen quietly at story time. At ever-younger ages, formal lessons are also being added to the assortment of skills children pick up simply by being together in a structured and nurturing environment.

Several generations ago, children learned to read in first grade. Now reading instruction usually begins in kindergarten. "So many people have complained that kindergarten standards have gotten tougher over the years," observes Elizabeth McGhee, who works with special needs preschoolers and has taught at a charter school in Atlanta. "If a child starts kindergarten without knowing all of their letters, letter sounds, and being able to write their name, they're already behind. The children are expected to be reading by the end of the school year. This puts a ton of pressure on parents and teachers."[1] Unfortunately, formal lessons leave children less time for unstructured play. By early grade school, recess may have been shortened or even disappeared entirely in some areas.

Some children thrive on the accelerated academic pace. They learn to read easily and move on to harder books. But others struggle. They may be as capable as the earlier readers but just not as emotionally ready to sit still and sound out words. Expectations are placed upon them that they are not ready to meet. The excited curiosity with which they began school begins to wane, and keeping up with lessons becomes a burden.

In the past decade, the focus on early achievement seems to have sped up even more. Serena Gersten noticed the trend in 2012. "When I was five, I played, had fun, and learned age-appropriate things," she wrote. "Unfortunately, that is not the case anymore. Now, the kindergarteners are expected to master things that I did not even learn until higher grades." Besides reading, she mentioned "analyz[ing] shapes and compos[ing] writing prompts."[2]

Serena's relatively carefree kindergarten experience hardly stunted her own academic progress. The well-reasoned, articulate article she wrote about early education was published in the *New York Times* when she was only in seventh grade. "There are just not

Some children are more advanced than others and may surge ahead of their classmates academically. Those who are not as accelerated can feel pressure to catch up.

enough hours and days in the school year," she wrote. "It is just too stressful."[3]

Dedicated and creative teachers do their best to make learning fun. Like Maria Mitchell, they want to see their students excited and self-motivated. New England teacher Michael Kenney developed an especially original way to teach reading. He turned a fly swatter into a word swatter. He names a word, and children take turns finding and swatting the word on an easel. The learning is punctuated with lots of laughter.

"I try to mix the fun and the lessons," said Kenney in an interview with Boston.com. "But we are testing them so much that I barely have time to teach the curriculum. These are five and six year olds, and there is so little time for them to be kids."[4]

Scripted Lessons

As children progress in elementary school, the workload gets heavier, especially around fourth or fifth grade. Maria Edmunds, an elementary school counselor in Northeast Pennsylvania, feels that many children begin to experience stress in third grade, when they face their first state-mandated assessment tests. Recently, attention has focused on the idea of tests controlling the curriculum. Lessons may be carefully scripted to maximize students' test results, a practice sometimes known as teaching to the test. This doesn't mean that the curriculum is adjusted to individual test items and concepts, Edmunds stresses. Rather, classroom instruction emphasizes the broad national standards on which students will be assessed.

Performance-based merit pay and job ratings based on their students' test performance have increased educators' anxieties. Teachers may become worried about how well their students will score and unintentionally pass their tension on to the children. "I have seen times when anxiety to do their best has gotten kids really worked up," said Edmunds. "We've had kids break down and cry."[5]

Edmunds' school has done away with art, music, and P.E. teachers for budgetary reasons. As teachers retire in these fields, they are not replaced. Regular classroom teachers have taken over the responsibility of teaching these subjects. The programs are not as comprehensive as they were when educational specialists directed them. Children miss out on a great deal of enrichment and fun, as well as the chance to develop their talents. In addition, as Edmunds points out, "[The arts and P.E.] are areas where kids with learning disabilities may shine or, at the very least, find fulfillment and enjoyment."[6] The activities can also go a long way toward helping them relax in more academic settings.

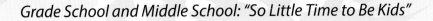

Many teachers are restricted by mandates from their school and state. They may be forced to focus on teaching to state standards instead of ensuring the comfort and success of their students.

Playing Is Learning: Global School Play Day

Recognizing children's needs to unwind and simply be kids, Tim Bedley, a fifth grade teacher at Earl Warren Elementary School in Lake Elsinore, California, created a movement called Global School Play Day. "Play is part of child development," said Bedley, who feels that young children experience a great deal of pressure.[7] "We want schools, parents, and community members to take note," he said. "Unstructured play is not a waste of time. It promotes initiative, creativity, problem solving skills, and a whole range of social skills."[8] More than sixty thousand children from eighteen countries participated in the first annual event, held on February 4, 2015. Because the need for play knows no age limits, students from middle and high school also took part.

Some teachers prepared their students by talking about imaginative ways in which they played in the 1960s, 1970s, or 1980s. Children were allowed to bring favorite toys to school with the exception of electronic devices or anything deemed a safety hazard. It was a time for spontaneity and creativity to flourish. Homework and tests could be forgotten for a day.

The Speech That Changed Education

A generation or two ago, elementary school went through sixth grade, after which students entered two years of junior high school. That began to change after 1963, when Dr. William Alexander gave a speech on education at Cornell University. He was supposed to talk about junior high schools, but while waiting for his plane to take off, he decided to make some drastic changes in his talk. He felt that the existing schools imposed an educational structure on intermediate students that was more appropriate for older teenagers. In his speech, Alexander proposed that "the concept of junior high schools be changed to middle schools that were designed to be more responsive to the needs and interests of young adolescents."[9] He wanted children of eleven to thirteen years old to have "more chances to participate in planning and managing their own activities, more resources for help on their problems of growing up, and more opportunities to explore new interests and develop new aspirations." The speech launched a movement in which middle schools quickly outpaced the older junior high schools in number.

Getting Ready for Middle School

The transition from elementary into middle school is one that many children anticipate eagerly. It's a time of new friendships and challenging new classes, of growing independence and responsibilities. Through a variety of optional and mandatory programs, middle schools try hard to make incoming sixth graders feel welcome and confident. One school in central Virginia offers a summer program given to groups of fifteen students at a time. Led by a teacher, the students learn their way around the school, figure out how to open the lockers, and get a preview of what it's like to change rooms and teachers for each subject. Perhaps most important of all, they get to know each other so they start the first day of school with a few ready-made new friends. Once the school year officially begins, the program is repeated in an abbreviated form.

Cesar Chavez Middle School in Oceanside, California, reaches out to students while they're still in fifth grade. Counselors visit their classrooms and answer questions. Later, the students will visit the school as a class. They will also be encouraged to join their parents for a special evening in May at their new school. To further ease the transition in August, sixth graders only have three or four teachers (one for language arts and history, one for math and science, one for an elective, and one for P.E.) instead of a different teacher for every subject. The hope is that fewer adjustments will lessen any stress a student may be feeling and help new sixth graders transition to their new middle school.

Finding a Balance

Even with the best orientation and supportive environment, the challenges of middle school can be daunting, as well as exciting.

Kids in middle school need to develop social skills, as well as staying afloat academically. This time is full of changes for students, and they may feel pressures they haven't faced before.

Pressures, both social and academic, mount. Students are growing and changing rapidly. At times, some may feel left out, confused, or lonely. "Middle school is about learning how to get along with people—learning how to make and keep friends," says counselor Gayle Hamilton of Cesar Chavez. She urges students "to build a support system [of parents, teachers, friends, etc.] and use it," emphasizing that such a network is "a biggie."[10] Every child needs someone to help him or her sort through problems or worries that may arise.

Social predicaments can affect a student's academic performance. Someone who is struggling to find friends may have a hard time paying attention in class or focusing on assignments. The more the student falls behind, the more anxious he or she becomes about getting a decent grade. But that anxiety may hinder the ability to concentrate.

Social relations affect schoolwork in another way, too. If a person's friends aren't interested in schoolwork, that student may lose interest, too. Homework and studying takes a backseat to texting classmates, visiting the mall, or playing video games. There's nothing wrong with such activities. They're part of the fun of growing up. But if they take up too much time, a student may fall behind in his or her classes. This can lead to a great deal of anxiety at report card time or the night before a big project is due.

At the other end of the spectrum are straight A students who are super-focused on their grades. Gayle Hamilton meets with such students every six weeks. In January, she often asks what New Year's resolutions they've made. The most common response is to maintain that perfect four-point average. "Do you have any fun resolutions?" Hamilton counters. "I want you to be well balanced."[11] She urges students not to be too disappointed if they don't do well on a test but to look for the bright spots that are part of every day.

Academic workloads begin to pile up in middle school, but at the same time, it's important to remember to have fun and be a kid.

A Student's Trajectory

Making time for relaxation, as well as work, is important for the mental and physical health of all students from grade school through college. Sometimes, however, tests, homework, and worries about grades get in the way of maintaining this crucial balance. Even though it's half a decade or more away, some students in middle school have begun thinking about college. According to seventh grade teacher Barbara Poole of Rachel Carson Middle School in northern Virginia, 60 percent of her students in 2015 already knew which college they wanted to attend.[12] Stephen M. Smith, a cofounder of a college prep subscription service, feels that the choices they make in middle school may help some of those students achieve their goals. For example, students, in collaboration with their parents and counselors, are asked to decide what math class to take. Their selection will affect what math they take in high school. A student who does not complete a year of algebra in middle school is unlikely to get to calculus by his or her senior year in high school, and calculus looks good on a college application.

Young people's choices, emphasizes Smith, "can really change their trajectory as a student."[13] But wait a minute, say others who are less concerned with the future implications of such choices than with children's emotional well-being. Making class choices so significant puts a great deal of pressure on eleven, twelve, and thirteen year olds, many of whom may not be looking that far into the future.

Once again, it's a fine line to draw. Should children do the things they enjoy, or should they focus on future goals? Where is the middle ground? On one hand, Rebecca Poole urges her students to compile a resume of activities. "It is competitive out there," she challenges them, "and what can you do other than going home and playing video games? You are twelve years old. Do you give back?" At the same time, however, she tells them not to forget "they are just kids."[14]

There's no road map on how to achieve the balance. Each student must find his or her own way.

High School: Menu of Options

The first day of high school is exciting and confusing as students attend half a dozen or so new classes and navigate crowded hallways in a sea of faces they don't recognize. The freedom and expectations of middle school have ratcheted up several notches. Most students welcome the greater independence, but the experience can also be a bit overwhelming. This is especially true if someone is attending a different school from most of his or her middle school classmates. And the pressure can start even before the first day.

Choosing Your High School

Traditionally, students from one middle school have attended the same high school together. In some areas, however, that has begun to change. Students are being asked to decide where they want to go to high school. In addition to private schools, the choices may include charter schools, magnet schools, STEM schools, or specialized schools that emphasize areas such as politics and international affairs, humanities, and the performing arts. In a process that mimics the college application process, students are required to fill out forms, get teacher recommendations, and provide transcripts. They may even be called in for an interview.

While some eighth graders and their parents may welcome the opportunity, for others the procedure is worrisome. "Many kids don't know what to do," reported a mother from Chesterfield County, Virginia, whose daughter "was intimidated by the whole process. It was anxiety provoking."[1] Ultimately, despite strong encouragement from her teachers, her daughter elected not to attend a specialty school. "I don't know what I want to be or do yet," she explained.[2] For those who do feel a strong pull toward a specific subject matter, however, Chesterfield County has twelve specialty centers and two technical centers.

AP or IB?

Wherever a student winds up attending high school, there are many more choices to make. In many schools, eligible students are encouraged to take Advanced Placement (AP) courses. These are college-level courses taught at the high school level. Students who do well in these classes get an added boost to their grade point average. For example, an A in a regular class equals four points. But an A in an AP class earns five points. To receive college credit, students must take an AP test at the end of the year. According to the College Board that oversees the AP program, almost fourteen thousand public high schools offered AP classes during the 2012-2013 academic year.[3]

In contrast, only eight hundred thirty schools in the United States offer courses in a smaller but growing program called the International Baccalaureate (IB).[4] Both the AP and IB offer intense learning experiences and college credit, but the scope of the courses differs. AP classes tend to concentrate on a specific topic while IB

Different Kinds of Schools

Charter Schools: Although publically funded, these elementary and secondary schools operate independently of the local school district. The charter that creates each school stipulates the educational programs, performance goals, and means of assessing those goals. Any group of people, such as parents, teachers, businesspeople, or even school districts, can submit a charter school proposal. Each state has a different entity in charge of authorizing charter schools. Charter schools that fail to meet their goals may be shut down.

Magnet Schools: Magnet schools specialize in themes, such as science and math, languages, fine and performing arts, and many others. Much of the learning takes place during hands-on projects. Although some magnet schools do not require applications, others designated as Talented & Gifted do ask for grades, test scores, and recommendations from parents or teachers. Magnet schools exist on both the elementary and secondary levels.

STEM Schools: Hands-on learning is the hallmark of STEM (Science, Technology, Engineering, Math) schools. As the number of science and technology jobs grows, interest in STEM schools has been growing, too. According to Kevin Bals, the principal of High Technology High School in New Jersey, the most important prerequisite is not necessarily an innate aptitude but a passion for the subject matter. "You have to want it," he told *U.S. News and World Report* in 2014. "If you want it, you will struggle through until you get it."[5]

classes tackle subjects from a broader perspective. Matthew Nelson of Metropolitan Nashville Public Schools in Tennessee explains the differing emphasis between the two programs. "In an AP class, you may look very deeply at an issue and look at it from multiple perspectives. In IB . . . you may be looking at an issue over time and how it has impacted other parts of the world and how there is that connectivity to it all."[6] Like their AP classmates, IB students take a year-end exam. Both programs look good on college applications.

"Standards Have Been Raised"

Whether or not they elect to do AP or IB classes, there's little doubt that college-bound students face more rigorous challenges than their parents did. "The standards that create pressure have been raised," explained Bryan Carr, a counselor at James River High School in Midlothian, Virginia. "For high-achieving kids, there is more pressure. We have the most well-prepared kids in the history of schooling. There's a price for that."[7]

More About the International Baccalaureate

The goal of the International Baccalaureate, founded in Geneva, Switzerland in 1968, is to prepare students for college and turn them into world citizens. In 2011, the nonprofit educational organization opened its four thousandth program in an international school in Wuxi, China. Students enrolled in an IB program can elect to earn an IB high school diploma that is acknowledged by colleges in all countries. As public awareness of our global community grows, so does interest in IB programs. "Forty years ago, international education was a 'nice to have,'" said Drew Deutsch, Director for IB's programs in the Americas. "Now, it's a necessity."[8]

For ambitious students, good grades take on immense importance as a requirement for getting into a prestigious college. Caught up in a materialistic society, some students and their parents see education as the key to earning power. These students fear that their whole future depends on getting into the best college possible. According to their reasoning, only a degree from an Ivy League university, such as Harvard or Yale, will guarantee them a top job in the field of their choice.

Retired teacher and children's author Paul Fleisher believes there are better ways to look at education. "School shouldn't just be preparation for future life," he cautions. "The things you do in school should be of value in and of themselves."[9]

No one wants classes to become a burden or compromise students' physical or mental well-being. However, a senior at a highly rated high school in Maryland probably spoke for many others when he said, "Everyone is stressed for the simple fact that we're not sure if we're working for our own passion and dreams or for other people's expectation."[10]

Pressure at All Levels

If the top students in high school are experiencing more stress, so are students at the opposite end of the spectrum. Minimum requirements for graduation have risen in many schools. More math, science, and social studies may be required than were a generation ago. For those students not as academically inclined as others, this can be a challenging course of study.

And what about the group in the middle? A great deal of attention is focused on high achievers and on students struggling for passing marks, but students in the middle who tend to get B and C grades also have to deal with stress. They also face hard classes, tests, and lots of homework. Vice Principal Jennifer Coleman of James River High School expresses concern that these students, many of whom could use help in developing abilities and study skills, are sometimes overlooked by busy counselors and teachers.

For every student who is anxious about not keeping up academically, there are just as many who feel the pressure to stay on top—to take the most advanced classes and to excel at them.

AVID—Help Students in the Middle

There are many reasons why students may fall in the middle range. Some B or C students have academic potential but lack organizational or study techniques that could boost their academic performance. Others from low socioeconomic backgrounds may lack the opportunities that some higher achieving students have enjoyed. Still others may be dealing with family issues, such as divorce or death that affect their schoolwork. AVID (Advancement Via Individual Determination) is a program that aims to help these students improve their skills and prepare for higher education.

More than two thousand schools in the United States offer AVID. Students apply as freshmen or sophomores and generally stick with the program throughout their high school years. "We have a wide range [of students]," said Sean McComb, who teaches English and AVID at Patapsco High School and Center for the Arts in Baltimore, Maryland. "They're all focused on this idea of fulfilling college dreams. And almost every student is first generation [in their family to attend college]."[11] By equipping these students with the tools they need to grow intellectually, study efficiently, and write well, AVID may reduce their anxieties, and at the same time it prepares them for success. McComb, the 2014 National Teacher of the Year, is gratified to see his former students go on to careers in education, nursing, and other important fields.

Preparing for Life

No one is immune to tension, including the teachers and counselors themselves. "The pressure is on educators," admits Coleman. "Therefore, the pressure is on students. [This] pressure to produce [academic] results overshadows the love of learning."[12]

But the excitement of exploring new ideas can never be totally quashed. Even while preparing students for standardized tests, most teachers strive to make their subjects interesting and relevant. And many students respond with enthusiasm and curiosity—perhaps not all the time but often enough to give them a satisfying sense of adventure. Although some stress is inevitable in high school, students who learn to handle it are preparing themselves for life.

Homework: Then and Now

Homework and backpacks go together like nuts and bolts. As any student knows, lots of homework usually means lots of books and a heavy, bulging backpack. Those attending schools that issue lightweight technology, such as laptops or tablets, may fare better, but the problem of overstuffed backpacks is widespread enough to attract major attention. The US Consumer Product Safety Commission notes that fourteen thousand children each year are treated for injuries related to their backpacks. Five thousand end up in emergency rooms.[1]

But apart from the literal heaviness of homework, there's an emotional weight, too. Popular author Bruce Feiler captured that aspect somewhat humorously in an article for the *New York Times*. "Just drop the word [homework] into any conversation with families and watch the temperature rise."[2] Like the shaggy-haired green "tuition monster" gobbles up money on a popular

TV commercial for insurance, excessive homework, say critics, gobbles up time, energy, and family fun. The question is when does it become excessive? How much homework is too much? Parents and educators have been seeking these answers for more than one hundred years.

A Law Against Homework!

The debate over homework is hardly new. In the 1880s, a former Civil War general named Francis Walker became fed up with the amount of homework his children did each night. He felt they were bored, tired, and overly worried about getting everything done. Many parents feel uncomfortable challenging the school system. But Walker was president of the school board in Boston. He convinced the board to limit the amount of homework a teacher could assign.[3]

It was not long before other people took up the crusade against homework, too. Some doctors claimed that homework kept children cramped indoors too much. It denied them the benefits of fresh air and exercise. A popular magazine, *Ladies' Home Journal*, also claimed that homework was a threat to good health.

The California legislature took such charges to heart. In 1901, it passed a law that prevented teachers from giving homework to students from kindergarten through eighth grade. The law also set limits on the amount of work that high school kids could be asked to do. Fifteen years later, there was little fuss when the law was revoked. Teachers were free to assign as much homework as they wanted.

The Progressive Movement

The war raged on as many people continued to fight the concept of homework. In 1930, the American Child Health Association called homework a major factor in rate of tuberculosis and heart disease among young people.[4] A new approach to schooling, the Progressive Movement, broadened the scope of education to include physical and emotional well-being, as well as academic achievement. Progressives thought it was more important for

Tips to Lighten the Load[5]

If your backpack is causing you pain or strain, here are a few tips from Children's Healthcare of Atlanta, Georgia, to help lessen the discomfort:

- Choose a backpack with two broad, padded shoulder straps.

- Don't carry unnecessary books or items in your backpack.

- At its heaviest, your backpack should not be more than 15 percent of your body weight.

- The heaviest books should go toward the back of backpack, or closest to your body.

- Bend your knees when picking up your loaded backpack and use both hands to hoist it to your shoulders.

- Yoga and weight training can strengthen the lower back and abdominal muscles that bear the weight of your backpack.

- A hiker's metal frame backpack or a bag on wheels can be good alternatives to traditional school backpacks, but check to make sure they are allowed by your school.

In the 1950s, the Space Race with Russia spurred a need for more rigorous education.

children to be healthy and lead well-rounded lives than to master school materials as quickly as possible. One Progressive went so far as to call homework for children in grade school and junior high "legalized criminality."[6]

Despite such opposition, homework didn't just disappear. Many parents still thought some homework was a good idea. In moderation, homework could help their children become eager and disciplined learners. Teachers continued to hand out some assignments, especially in the upper grades. But according to a national survey, most high school students in 1948 spent less than an hour a night on homework.[7]

Sputnik Changes Education

In 1957, the world entered a new era, the Space Age, when what was then the Soviet Union launched the first artificial satellite, *Sputnik*. Competition was fierce between the United States and Communist Russia during the period after World War II known as the Cold War. Many Americans were shocked and alarmed that the Russians beat this country into space. People began to worry that Russian schools were turning out better scientists and engineers than American schools. There seemed only one way to remedy this situation. Students would have to study more science and math. To many educators, this also meant that they would have to do more homework.

A Nation at Risk

Even though students were spending extra time on after-school studies, some educators thought they weren't doing enough. In 1983, a government publication titled *A Nation at Risk* concluded that children were not being adequately challenged or prepared for the future. The study compared US schools unfavorably with schools in foreign countries. Bluntly it stated "that for too many people education means the minimum work necessary for the moment." Some of the language was even stronger. "If an unfriendly foreign power had attempted to impose on America the mediocre educational performance that exists today," stated the report, "we might well have viewed it as an act of war."[8] Stringent reforms were called for, including more rigorous standards, increased homework, an extended school day, and a longer school year. Educators took these recommendations seriously as the "tougher standards" movement gained acceptance across the country.[9] Teachers began assigning more homework. In 1995, an editorial in a major magazine said that homework was the closest thing possible to "a one word solution to America's educational problems."[10]

Continuing Controversy

The debate over homework is not likely to end any time soon. Some educators feel that a strict homework policy is the hallmark of a quality education. Others feel that intense homework interferes with a child's personal growth. Each child is a unique individual, they reason. Each has his or her own emotional and intellectual needs. Demanding the same homework from all students is a misguided attempt to fit all children into a single mold. Which group is correct? The arguments are strong from both sides.

Taming the Homework Monster

No one wants to say up past midnight doing homework, but that's what some students report doing. According to a survey of more than four thousand students from high-performing California high schools, students averaged more than three hours of homework a night. That doesn't leave much time for other things. "[Homework] takes me away from everything I used to do," complained one participant in the survey.[1] "There's never a break. Never," said another.[2] Students have to decide what is most important to them. Do they want to play sports? Practice a musical instrument? Spend time with a younger sibling? Hang out with friends? The list goes on. A myriad of activities compete for attention. But there are many reasons to make homework a top priority.

Homework: The Pros

Doing assignments outside of school crams more learning into a single day, argue proponents of homework. It enables students to master material and acquire needed skills more quickly. Tightly packed schedules seldom allot enough time to write a story, solve algebra problems, or research the life of Albert Einstein during the school day. But these are activities worth doing. Without homework, classes would not be as challenging or rewarding.

But homework does more than help a student understand his or her studies. According to many educators, it builds character, too. It teaches students to be persistent, determined, and disciplined. It gives them a sense of accomplishment for a job well done. Students feel proud of a well-written report or of solving the problems in a math assignment. And they actually learn more. In this way, homework boosts confidence. It also teaches students to budget time carefully, which is an essential skill for life in the real world. Champions of homework say that all these benefits are worth the pastimes students may be forced to sacrifice.

Homework: The Cons

Can there be too much of a good thing? Most young people would respond with a resounding yes. At some time or other almost every student has complained about too much homework. But teachers, eager to present necessary information and skills, keep heaping on assignments. When children have more than one teacher, the problem may be compounded. Nobody wants to do twenty math problems and write an English essay the night before a big science test. When assignments pile up in this way, homework becomes an excessive burden. Students become tense and anxious. They lose the joy of learning and may become resentful if they have to give up activities that they love doing. Parents, called upon to help their children with homework, can also become stymied by the amount and difficulty of homework.

A Good Night's Rest

When students are saddled with too much homework, they often lose sleep. The later they stay up, the less alert they become. The next day at school, they are likely to be too tired to concentrate. The brain simply can't focus effectively on history or science or algebra problems. Insufficient sleep can also lead to irritability and mood swings.

A survey conducted by the National Sleep Foundation in 2014 found that children of all ages are not getting the recommended amount of sleep, which is nine to twelve hours for students in grade school and middle school and eight to ten hours for teenagers. More than a quarter of all teenagers have fallen asleep in school at

Two Sides to Homework

On the **PLUS** side, **HOMEWORK** . . .

- Enables you to master material more quickly
- Gives you a sense of accomplishment
- Helps build character and gives you a chance to develop persistence and confidence
- Fosters time management skills
- Helps you get into a good college
- Prepares you to face the rigors of the real world

On the **MINUS** side, **HOMEWORK** . . .

- Can sometimes be mere busy work
- Can cause you to get insufficient sleep
- Leaves you less time for family and social activities
- Creates stress and anxiety
- Can contribute to student burnout
- May not be as effective a learning tool as some teachers think

The goal of teachers and students everywhere is to maximize the pluses and decrease the negatives.

Stress can get in the way of a good night's sleep, yet being well rested is essential for good health and academic performance. Try not to stay up too late, and stay away from electronic devices before bed.

some time. Many have also fallen asleep doing their homework. "I encourage [my students] not to stay up until two or three in the morning," says Jeffrey Doyle, an AP teacher at James River High School, "They still do."[3] But by helping kids build the skills they need to succeed in school and by making himself available for questions via email, Doyle strives to lessen academic worries and enable his students to finish homework with enough time for a good night's sleep.

Electronic devices also play a role in the sleep dilemma. Approximately three quarters of children have an electronic device, such as a television, laptop, or smart phone, in their bedroom. Because these devices stimulate the brain, they hinder the ability to sleep. Students who use electronics late at night or leave a device on when they go to bed lose an average of half an hour of sleep. Although this doesn't sound like much, it can have a profound effect on how they feel the next day.

When high school students stay up late to study, they naturally do not feel like getting up in the morning. There is another reason, however, that they may want to stay in bed. This has to do with their circadian rhythm. Like a form of biological clock, the circadian rhythm dictates when someone sleeps and awakens. As children become adolescents, their circadian rhythm changes so they can't sleep easily before 11:00 P.M. To get the amount of sleep they need, they have to sleep later in the morning. But this is an impossibility for many teens because their schools start so early.

ZZZ's to A

Since 1998, Congresswoman Zoe Lofgren from California has repeatedly tried to remedy this situation by introducing a bill, appropriately called the ZZZ's to A Act into Congress. The measure would encourage high schools to delay opening until 9:00 A.M. Schools willing to accept later opening and closing times would receive special funding. "I first became aware of this issue with my own children," Lofgren said in 2014. "As my oldest child became a teenager, she went from early bird to a youngster who was very difficult to get out the door to school in the morning—bleary-eyed and overtired."[4] Although the proposed legislation has failed to pass Congress several times, Lofgren considers it important enough to keep reintroducing it.

Later school hours would mean less time at the end of the day for homework, but the gain in student well-being could make the trade-off worth it. Also vitally important, the measure could lessen the risk of students driving when they are exhausted and risking serious injury. According to Dr. Judith Owens of the American Academy of Pediatrics, "The research is clear that adolescents who get enough sleep have a reduced risk of being overweight or suffering depression, are less likely to be involved in automobile accidents, and have better grades, higher standardized test scores, and an overall better quality of life."[5]

Although most high schools continue to open early, a few have decided to experiment with later hours. Studies indicate that the change paid big dividends in terms of student achievement and emotional health. Grades tended to go up while stress levels went down.[6]

Homework Tips

Some students have a confident attitude toward homework. They expect to get their assignments done and do them well. Other students may be just as capable, but they handle stress poorly. They worry about how much they have to do and yearn for some free time simply to unwind. The challenge is to maximize the good effects of homework and eliminate the bad. Luckily, there are many things that all middle and high school students can do to keep homework from becoming too demanding. Here are some tips to keep in mind when you're dealing with homework:

> **Choose courses carefully.** Be careful when you're signing up for courses. It's good to challenge yourself, but leave yourself some leeway, too. You don't have to take all the hardest classes.

The most successful people are also the most organized people. Write down assignments and other activities in a planner or type them into your phone so nothing comes as a surprise.

Discuss your class schedule carefully with your counselor and your parents. They will help you decide what's realistic for you. You might want to arrange your day so you have at least one class that doesn't require a great deal of daily homework. This could be your chance to try something new, such as drama or pottery or music lessons. It could also be an opportunity to unwind and relax in the middle of your school day.

Get a homework game plan. When your teacher gives a homework assignment, pay close attention. Make certain you know exactly what he or she wants. It helps if you write everything down in a planner. All sorts of scheduling helpers are available in office supply stores. Choose one with a calendar that leaves plenty of space to write down each day's assignments. Or create your own planner on a computer or tablet. Estimate the amount of time you will need for each assignment, and write that down, too. Be generous. Don't plan to write an English essay in ten minutes or build a model of the solar system in the half hour before you go to bed. And be sure to allow yourself plenty of breaks.

Don't wait until the last minute. Putting off your homework as long as possible often backfires. You may run out of time and energy. You may end up cheating yourself on sleep. Or you may end up in class without your homework. The latter situation is not the end of the world, but it can be stressful.

Seek help if necessary. Almost everyone has trouble with homework at some time or other. As writer and educator Alfie Kohn points out in his book, *The Schools Our Children Deserve*, "No one can learn very effectively without making mistakes and without bumping up against limits."[7] Challenging assignments help you to expand the boundaries of your knowledge and skills.

After you've tried your best and still find a particular assignment too hard, ask a parent, grandparent, older sibling, or classmate for help. If you're still having a problem, do as much of the assignment

Parents can be extremely helpful when it comes to homework assignments. To decrease frustration, give them plenty of time to brush up on the subject if necessary.

as you can, then put it out of your mind. Now might be a good time to take a walk, practice a musical instrument, or call up a friend. The next day you can explain the situation to the teacher and ask for more help.

Studying for a Test

Not all homework is written, of course. Sometimes when you're studying for a test, it can seem that your homework will never be done. How can you tell when you know enough? Might an extra hour of study make the difference between an A and a B? Test anxiety blows everything out of proportion. It can lessen your concentration and actually make you score less well on the test. One student who

Don't let school make you physically sick. If you are studying too hard, make sure you take a break and get some fresh air and exercise. If you are stressed, talk to someone about your anxieties.

suffers from test anxiety explained her frustration to educator and writer Denise Clark Pope. "When I'm studying I get, like, really very nervous, and then I get a stomachache, and I get so I can't study no more.... Then when I get to the test, I fail because I haven't studied! I can't remember anything. I am just blank and can't think."[8]

Another student, now a high school teacher, recalls panicking during math tests in high school. "I'd realize I wasn't doing the problems right. It made me physically ill."[9]

If this scenario sounds familiar, you should discuss your symptoms with your parents and teacher. There is no need for you to become sick or over-agitated about any test. A counselor may offer techniques to help you relax or think more clearly under pressure.

Perhaps some accommodations can be worked out by allowing you more time for the test or a chance to take a break and walk around.

You can also fight test anxiety by studying smart—that is, by organizing your time and materials. You might start by listing the page numbers you need to review and separating the class notes you have to go over. When you know exactly what you have to cover, it won't seem so overwhelming. Concentrate on the major points, then decide what details you should learn. If you start to feel stressed, take a break. Exercise is a good way to break through your apprehension. It's hard to feel negative when you're walking or running or riding your bike. Go into the test relaxed, rested, and ready to do your best.

6

High Stakes Tests and How They Got Started

Ankur Singh was supposed to taking his French AP exam. But he was tired of taking tests and angry that so much of his education revolved around preparing for tests. So instead of answering his French questions, he used the test booklet to write a letter to the College Board. Later he was called to the school office, where he found his high school French teacher waiting for him. Singh steeled himself for the trouble he was about to face. To his relief, however, his French teacher sympathized with him and explained that she, too, was tired of spending so much class time drilling students for tests. "And then," recalled Singh later, "my French teacher said something that I won't forget for a long time. 'Maybe if the students themselves spoke out against [standardized testing], it could change.' So that's what I did."[1]

In college, Singh took a semester off to film a 106-minute documentary, *Listen: The Movie*, in which he gave students a chance to vent their feelings about testing. "They never ask us students what we want from our own education," said Singh in 2013, when he was nineteen. "And since we are the primary stakeholders, that is not okay."[2] Singh's film ends with video clips of students protesting the extreme emphasis on standardized testing in Chile; Quebec; Portland, Oregon; and Chicago, Illinois. Perhaps some who saw the film would have liked to join in.

Establishing Standards

Standardized tests have not always been accorded such a prominent place in education. Much of today's preoccupation with standardized testing dates back to the 1983 publication of *A Nation of Risk*. The scathing indictment of American education shocked elected officials and businesspeople across the country. Some governors and legislatures began to consider the idea of establishing standards to be followed by all the schools in their state. In 1990, Maryland became the first state to adopt such a system. One year later, the state instituted a test to be taken by students in various grades.[3] Soon other states followed suit. The era of widespread standardized tests had begun.

No Child Left Behind

When George W. Bush was inaugurated president in 2001, he had strong ideas about improving the nation's educational system. Bush felt that tests were the best way to judge how well or how poorly schools were doing their jobs. He wanted the results to be tabulated so schools could track the progress of minority students and low-income children. Children in such groups often scored below their more affluent classmates. Bush wanted to make certain that all children got an excellent education and met certain goals. Schools whose students did not make yearly gains would have to institute improvements. But if their changes did not result in higher test scores, the schools would lose federal funding. If scores continued

The US government standardized public education to raise academic levels, but critics complain these measures result in teaching to the test.

to lag behind the acceptable standard, eventually the school could be shut down.

Ultimately 90 percent of the country's senators and representatives voted for Bush's plan. On January 2, 2002, the president signed the No Child Left Behind Act (NCLB) into law. "As of this hour, America's schools will be on a new path of reform and a new path of results," Bush declared.[4]

Although the new law included many provisions, the most important one stipulated that all children in grades three through eight be tested yearly in reading and math. Each state was to adopt its own exams. Students were to be tested at least once in high school. The fate of every school and its staff depended on whether test scores showed adequate yearly progress (AYP). The original goal was for every child to pass the tests by 2014. Unfortunately, most schools did not reach that milestone.

Common Core

The tests mandated by NCLB highlighted an interesting discrepancy. In certain states, students did well on their assessment exams but scored poorly on national college board tests, such as the SAT or ACT.[5] In other states, there was little or no disparity between scores on national and state tests. Had they received a better education? The Common Core movement gained momentum as an attempt to remedy this situation so children receive the same high quality education wherever they live.

Even before NCLB, however, the National Governors' Association and other organizations had taken steps to raise national standards for all American schools. After much research by a coalition of states, the Common Core State Standards were released in June 2010. These include learning objectives in math and English for kindergarten through high school. Although the Common Core originated with the states, many people connect it with President Obama because his administration offered federal funds to states that adopted the standards. As of 2015, forty-six states, as well as the

District of Columbia, have accepted the Common Core Standards. Assessing how well students have mastered the standards begins in third grade and satisfies the NCLB Act's requirement of yearly assessments.

"A Lot of Pressure From Different Directions"

The No Child Left Behind Act has been up for renewal by Congress since 2007. Both political parties agree that the law needs to be revised. As former governors or state legislators, many Congressmen have dealt firsthand with problems in the NCLB act. Others have received complaints from the voters. "There's a lot of pressure from a lot of different directions to finally get this done," said Patrick McGuinn of Drew University in Madison, New Jersey.[6] But Republicans and Democrats have yet to agree on exactly how the law should be amended. On February 27, 2015, the House of Representatives elected not to vote on a proposed revision of the law titled the Student Success Act.

Teaching to the Test

Advocates of standardized tests say that they motivate both teachers and children. Teachers focus on the most important things children

Opting Out

Some parents, as well as educators, feel that too many tests are eating up valuable school time and causing many students needless anxiety. In a growing protest, many families are deciding not to have their children take the Common Core tests. According to *The New York Times*, most states have movements in which parents decide their children will opt out. "I'm refusing [to have my children take the test] because we're taking a stand against this deeply flawed policy," said Christine McGoey who helped organize some protest events in New Jersey. "I feel the only thing left to do is just say no."[7]

High school students are inundated with important standardized tests. Knowing that their performance on these tests will impact the rest of their lives creates intense pressure on them.

need to learn. Students work hard to pass the tests. Students make giant leaps in knowledge and skills as evidenced by their high test scores. Other people believe there are more effective things than tests to help students learn and to prepare them for life. One of the most important is to reduce class size. Smaller classes mean students get more individual attention. The teacher can respond more readily to their questions and developmental needs.

Teachers are feeling the pressure to perform as well as students. Their jobs and government funding for their schools depend on how well their students score on standardized tests. In their anxiety, teachers may focus their lessons to materials covered on the test. In other words, they end up teaching to the test. One grade school principal put it simply: "What gets taught is what gets tested."[8] Some schools have cut way back on subjects such as art, music, and P.E. Even subjects that are considered more academic, such as history, science, and geography, have been curtailed in some places. This trend deprives children of a great deal of basic knowledge, as well as enriching experiences. As one teacher remarked, "How are we going to have informed citizens if they never learn social studies?"[9]

David Elkind had some things to say almost thirty years ago about the growing emphasis on tests:

> *Management programs, accountability, and test scores are what schools are about today and children know it. They have to produce or else. The pressure may be good for many students, but it is bound to be bad for those who can't keep up. Their failure is more public and therefore more humiliating than ever before. Worse, students who fail to achieve are letting down their peers, the principal, the superintendent, and the school board. This is a heavy burden for many children to bear and is a powerful pressure to achieve early and to grow up fast.*[10]

Test Anxiety

Despite such views, the importance of standardized tests is conveyed to students over and over. In some schools, they are primed like

When you have a test coming up, make sure you're prepared by studying in advance. Get plenty of rest the night before. Eat a healthy breakfast the morning of the test. And relax!

athletes prior to a big game. Their opponent is the test; their job is to conquer it. They are drilled continuously. They take one or more practice tests. In some places, they even sing pep songs. Under these circumstances, even the best-prepared students are bound to feel nervous. Students less likely to do well may be considerably more agitated. "The whole atmosphere of the school changes [on standardized test days]," noted one mother of an eighth grader. "Everybody's stressed. I just think it's counterproductive."[11]

Tension before a big test may be a bit like stage fright. Most actors say that some stage fright is normal and that it actually enhances their performance. Too much stage fright, however, has the opposite effect. It may paralyze the actor, cause him or her to mumble lines or miss cues, or focus on the audience instead of the characters on stage. In the same way, a little anxiety before a test may help keep you mentally alert. Too much apprehension can block your ability to concentrate and make it difficult for you to remember things.

There is a biological basis for this phenomenon. Author and educator Leslie Hart has studied the human brain and concluded that excessive anxiety indeed impairs a student's ability to learn. Excessive stress causes a person's brain to shift into a lower gear. This means that the brain cannot process information as effectively. According to authors and researchers Renate Nummela Caine and Geoffrey Caine, students should aim for "relaxed alertness."[12] Such a state of mind, calm but eager, frees students to do their best work.

Besides studying for a test, it's a good idea for students to prepare physically and psychologically. They should get plenty of sleep the night before, and eat a good breakfast. It's also wise to refrain from studying or talking about the test at the last moment. This helps a student clear his or her head and go into the test with a calm attitude.

If a student finds himself or herself stressing out in the middle of a test, he or she should take a few deep breaths. It can help to take a moment to put things in perspective. Anyone who starts to feel ill should tell a teacher.

Tests are merely tools. They measure knowledge but not what a student will do with that knowledge. They do not predict the enthusiasm or imagination that any individual will bring to his or her future.

Getting Into College

As we have seen, today's schools aim to give every student the tools needed to succeed in college. But it wasn't always this way. In the early twentieth century, only 4 percent of young people attended college.[1] High school graduation was the gateway to adulthood, jobs, and often marriage and families. By contrast, in 2014, 70 percent of high school students attended college immediately after high school.[2]

That doesn't mean, however, that a college diploma is essential to a happy, productive life, as the careers of many notables testify. Billionaire Bill Gates, founder of Microsoft, left Harvard his sophomore year because he "realized the error of [his] ways and decided [he] could make do with a high school diploma."[3] Another Harvard dropout, Mark Zuckerberg, went on to continue the work he had started in his dorm room. If you don't recognize his name, you'll certainly recognize his accomplishment, Facebook. Of course, these two examples are in a league by themselves. In general, college graduates do have broader job options and make more money than those without a diploma. But there are many people who lead productive, fulfilling lives without going to college.

Economic opportunity and professional aspirations, however, are only one reason why students decide to go to college. A college education gives someone a chance to sample different academic disciplines. It helps him or her acquire self-awareness and knowledge of the world. The experiences you have both in and out of the classroom may help you decide what you want to do with your life.

Taking Competition to a Whole New Level

Getting into a prestigious college is the dream of many high school students—a dream often carefully nurtured and sometimes even instilled by their parents. The problem, of course, is the number of applicants to the nation's top colleges and universities. More students want to go to big name schools than those schools have slots available. As we have seen, some students feel they have to do everything perfectly to win one of those slots. They must take the hardest classes and get all As. They must take part in a broad spectrum of extracurricular activities, including sports and student government. Their SAT scores must be astronomical, their class ranking number one, and their college essays polished and flawless.

Students who demand perfection of themselves are certain to feel overburdened at some time. All the hype surrounding college admissions doesn't help matters. Books abound on how to apply to college. Special courses promise the skills to ace entrance exams. Private counseling companies, which can cost many thousands of dollars, offer to help students present themselves in the best light to college admissions officers. College rankings in news magazines generate increased applications for the top rated schools.

While some tension is inevitable, college-bound seniors do not have to focus all their energy on the application process. There are many college options available for students of varied academic

Receiving two or three college catalogs every week can be overwhelming. Deciding which school will be the best fit for you is one of the most important choices you'll make in your lifetime.

records. These are fine institutions that offer a wide array of opportunities. The challenge and excitement comes in finding the college that's a right match for you.

College applications take competition to a whole new level. Most, if not all, public high schools rank students according to their grade point average (GPA). Since class ranking is used to determine the valedictorian and salutatorian, many students place great value on where they fall in the class hierarchy. They want the recognition of being number one, as well as the advantage they feel this will give them in the college application process. But the difference between number one and number two, or number twenty-nine and thirty for

The entire college application process can create stress because filling out applications forces you to assess your own academic performance.

that matter, can be as little as one thousandth of a point. Students and parents have even been known to sue school districts over class rankings.

Of course, most people would argue that a miniscule fraction of a point or the difference between the number one and number two class ranking isn't significant. Students can rank well below the top ten or twenty percent and still have excellent grades and be considered high achievers. But lawsuits show the intensity of the pressure that some students are feeling. They feel they must do something extraordinary to make themselves stand out among thousands and thousands of college applicants. In reality, however, a small difference in class ranking is unlikely to make any difference in the college admission process.

College Entrance Exams

One hurdle many students dread as they apply to college is facing the exams that most colleges require. The best known is the Scholastic Aptitude Test (SAT). Called by Alexandra Robbins "the most feared test in the United States," the SAT is supposed to measure aptitude or potential for learning.[4] Other tests called achievement tests measure how much a student has learned in a particular subject, such as chemistry or French.

Most students sign up to take the PSAT, or the preliminary test, in their sophomore year. This gives them an idea of how well they will do on the actual test in their junior year. If the score is disappointing, there's time to figure out what went wrong and to practice the different kinds of verbal and math questions. Some students find special preparation classes helpful, but these classes certainly aren't essential to scoring well. Even if the final score isn't what the student hoped for, there are still many good schools ready to consider his or her application. The SAT is simply one of several tools college admissions officers use to get to know applicants.

Test-Optional Schools

Admissions officers at some colleges are beginning to say they don't need scores to figure out if their college is right for a particular student. Although most schools still require some form of entrance exam, a sizeable number have made such tests optional. Among them are such top-rated schools as Bowdoin College and American University. As of July 2014, one US college, Hampshire College in Amherst, Massachusetts, was operating test blind, meaning that standardized tests scores have no place in its decisions.[5] The admissions office will not look at any test scores that are submitted. According to Hampshire's Dean of Admissions and Financial Aid Meredith Twombly, test scores are a "very poor indicator of success."[6]

Besides reducing anxiety on already stressed high school seniors, officials at test-optional schools hope the measure will help equalize opportunities from different backgrounds. Bob Schaeffer, a public education director for Fair Test, an organization that encourages the test-optional policy, explained to *USA Today*, "Low income kids don't have the same chances to sign up for expensive test prep courses that start at $1000, and their families don't have the resources to pay for them to take the SAT three or four or five times to boost their score."[7]

Time for Choices

College-bound students must cram a great deal into the first semester of their senior year. Most college applications are due by the end of the calendar year. It's time to make some hard decisions. To which colleges should the students apply? How many applications are necessary? What about financial aid? Should they apply for early decision at their top choice? Early decision, increasingly popular among some students, lets an individual know whether he or she has been admitted to a college several months before the general pool of applicants receives such information. Someone who is not accepted may be deferred. This means he or she will be considered

Just thinking about taking the SAT can make the heart rates of most high school students increase. For many colleges, SAT scores are less important than academic performance and extracurricular activities.

again with other candidates. If a student is accepted, he or she is obligated to attend that college.

Completing the applications is time consuming, although applying to some schools that use the Common Application, or Common App, may lessen the burden somewhat. In 2013, more than eight hundred thousand students used the online system to make 3.4 million college applications.[8] But the Common App site has been known to crash at the time when students need it the most. Although the problems seem to have been ironed out, it's best to start the process early. "You don't want to be scrambling in the zero hour," cautions Katherine Cohen, who founded an admissions consultancy agency in New York. "The students least affected by

Today, there are so many different colleges and universities with a wide spectrum of requirements applicants must meet. This means that nearly everyone can go on to college.

the Common App's technical troubles were those who started early and had plenty of time to troubleshoot issues before the application deadlines."[9]

Senior Year Stress

Even as they complete their applications, some students may also be boning up to take the SAT a second or even third time. Meanwhile, school doesn't stop just because some seniors are applying to college. Although the junior year is generally considered the toughest, seniors face heavy course loads that may include calculus, physics, advanced language, and history classes. Colleges will want to see the grades they get in these courses before making final decisions.

"We are a pretty stressed-out generation," Ryann Stibor, a high school senior from California, told CBS News. "It is a lot harder and becomes pretty cut-throat in high school. Everyone is competing for one spot in all these different schools—the one scholarship."[10] The intense concentration on a single goal leaves little time for relaxation. A survey conducted by the University of California at Los Angeles (UCLA) in 2014 found that high school seniors spent more time studying and less time with friends than students in 1987.[11] Psychologists fear that lack of socializing could lead to more stress and to depression.

Good News

If college applications are beginning to sound scary, there's plenty of good news to counteract student anxiety. The best news is that there are many fine colleges actively recruiting students. These institutions may not have instant name recognition, but they provide a good education and produce happy and successful graduates. If a student wants to go to college and is willing to work hard, he or she is almost certain of being accepted. But working hard does not mean a student has to take all AP classes or have a straight A average. No one has to be a super-studentwho juggles several extra curricular activities after school and arrives home exhausted. It's not even

Timeless Wisdom

Marion Sammartino, the author's mother, was an award-winning teacher and the popular author of a long-running newspaper column on education that ran in the 1980s and 1990s. Although schools have changed since then, her advice on academic success and the need for a balanced life is as relevant today as when she wrote it. Here is her advice to second semester high school seniors from a column that ran in 1999:

> At this time of the school year, we find many high school seniors anxiously awaiting responses to their applications for college admissions. It would be foolish for parents, teachers, and friends to ignore the anxiety imposed on these seniors.
>
> The process doesn't seem fair in that the last year of high school, which should be fun-filled and joyous, is really not. However, in time only the best will be remembered, and that is fortunate. New loyalties and friendships will develop at the colleges, and the admission process may become something to joke about. . . . College applicants should keep in mind that it is a known and proven fact that a college admission or a college rejection in no way diminishes or even enhances one's innate ability to be the very best in whatever they wish to accomplish.[12]

Marion Sammartino

necessary to be one of the top-ranked students in the senior class or make the honor roll every semester. All of these are wonderful accomplishments that may lead to a prestigious college. But if a student's goal is simply to get a good education at a solid institution, he or she can relax a bit. "We are well able to meet the needs of all of our children who want to go to college," affirms guidance counselor Bryan Carr.[13] A student's future does not depend on attending one of the so-called Ivy League schools.

Writing the Application

Senior year should be a time for fun, as well as work. Although it's normal to be a little nervous when applying to colleges, a few simple guidelines will help you minimize your stress.

Give yourself choices. Discuss with your parents and guidance counselor what you hope to get out of college. It's not unheard of for students to apply to a dozen or more colleges. This may lead to more options, but it's a huge job. And it's not necessary. A good rule of thumb is to divide your applications among three kinds of schools. Start with one or two stretch schools. These are highly competitive colleges where your chances of acceptance are smaller than at other good places. That's why they are called stretch schools—your admission is something of a stretch or a long shot. But if a particular school appeals to you, don't be afraid to apply. You may get in, after all. And even if you don't, you'll know that you did your best.

If you like, you may skip stretch schools altogether. The next applications are for schools that will likely accept you—strong possibilities. Counselors at James River High School in Midlothian, Virginia, call these competitive schools. Your GPA and test scores are comparable to those of students already in attendance, so you are competitive with them. If you end up attending a school from this group, you should be pleased.

Finally, you should not neglect what are sometimes called safety net schools. These are colleges that are certain to take you. Having a safety net takes some of the worry out of the application process.

Being accepted to your first choice is a great feeling. However, it is wise to apply to at least one school that you are virtually assured of getting into. This will decrease your stress level considerably.

And these schools provide an excellent education. So do two-year community colleges. These local institutions accept everyone with a minimum GPA. Students can live at home and save money if they opt for a community college. When they graduate with an A.A. (Associate of Arts) degree, they may apply to four-year colleges or look for jobs.

Don't succumb to peer pressure. This is not the time to compete with classmates. It's natural to talk about college with your friends, but try to avoid comparisons. One student's stretch school may be another student's competitive school. An especially outstanding student may include schools in his or her safety net that others have placed on their reach list. Your guidance counselor will help you decide what's realistic for you. Whatever your choices, be happy with them and attack the application process with enthusiasm. Don't feel pressured to apply to a big name school simply because some of your friends may be doing so. What's right for them may not be what's right for you.

Keep a calendar. Note the date when each of your applications is due. But create your own deadlines in advance of these. Decide when you want to have a first draft of your college essays done. Write that down, as well as appointments you make with your English teacher or counselor to go over the essays. Then note when you want each individual essay to be complete. Give yourself a due date for each aspect of your applications. Be sure to allot yourself plenty of time, and be realistic about all the other things you have to do. Scheduling your applications in this way will make the whole job of getting into college feel more manageable. When the last application is mailed, you can celebrate.

Don't expect to get into every college on your list. Of course, it's disappointing to receive a rejection letter. But many factors come into play when admissions officers are choosing future students. There are some factors you have no control over, such as the school's directive for geographic or ethnic diversity. And it's often difficult to get into a popular state school, such as the University of Virginia or one of the University of California campuses, if you do not live in that state.

Not gaining admittance to a particular college does not mean that you are less capable or that you will be less successful than the students who were admitted. Many famous individuals recall not being admitted to top name universities. These include Secretary of State John Kerry and television personality Meredith Vieira, who were both rejected by Harvard.[14] Mom and educator Mickey VanDerwerker puts things in perspective when she says, "It's not so much where you go to school [that counts] as what you take with you."[15]

8

When Stress Becomes Overwhelming

Everyone knows that a sharp rise in blood pressure is not a good thing. It stresses the body and can lead to serious heart conditions. A sudden drop in blood pressure is also a bad sign that can lead to dizziness, fainting spells, and excessive fatigue. There is a normal blood pressure between these extremes that is conducive to good health and optimal for everyone. A critical balance is also necessary with other kinds of pressures—including academic. Too little pressure can lead to aimlessness and lack of accomplishment. Too much pressure, however, can cause even the most ambitious students to shut down.

Unlike healthy blood pressure that remains in the same range for everyone, the right level of academic pressure varies from person to person. Juggling assignments is anxiety provoking for some students. The more these students have to do, the more nervous they become. Other students thrive on more stress. It sharpens their efficiency and perhaps gives them a competitive edge. But high or low, everyone has a level at which stress begins to exert a negative rather than a positive effect.

Excessive pressure extracts a physical and mental toll. People may cry or become angry more easily. They may suffer from headaches or stomachaches. People have even been known to temporarily lose their hair due to intense psychological pressure. Students are not immune to the serious consequences of stress. Destructive consequences of severe academic pressure include burnout, cheating, eating disorders, and substance abuse. In the most extreme cases, students have been known to harm themselves or attempt to end their lives.

Burnout

No one can work at peak efficiency all the time. Everyone needs some down time—that is, time to relax, listen to music, to do anything, or nothing at all. The hectic pace of modern education and after-school commitments makes this almost impossible for some students. Every minute is structured or spoken for. When an eighth grader or tenth grader has no chance to unwind, school may seem like a hardship with no relief in sight. It's hard to stay motivated under such circumstances. Somehow school no longer seems worth the effort. Faced with a mountain of homework, the student may feel paralyzed. The effort required to complete all his or her tasks no longer seems worth it. This condition is called burnout.

Students suffering from burnout are likely to let schoolwork slide. Worse that than, they lose their enthusiasm for learning. Completing an assignment does not seem worth the effort. Their tolerance for stress decreases, and they may become depressed. As these students fall behind in their studies and their grades drop, their anxiety increases in a downward spiral.

Depression has become all too common in modern society. Adults and younger people suffering from depression experience fatigue and a loss of interest in things they formerly enjoyed. They

Studying hard for long periods of time can work for a while—until you get burned out. Burnout can take a toll on your health and can negatively affect your schoolwork. To avoid burnout, be sure to take plenty of breaks and make time for other activities.

feel sad and dread facing the day. Routine jobs or schoolwork may loom as formidable tasks. It's not easy to get over depression or burnout alone, but there is always help available. If intense pressure has caused you to lose your motivation, the following guidelines may help you on the road back to your former, more energetic self.

Remember you are not alone. Many students have felt exactly as you do. They have managed to complete their classes successfully and regain their energy. You can too!

You do not have to be a super-student. It's better to be healthy and happy than to get straight As. "If you don't get an A, that doesn't mean you're not capable," points out English teacher Autumn Nabors.[1]

Share your feelings with an adult you trust. This could be a parent, counselor, or therapist. Explain that you can't muster up your old interest in your classes, and you wonder if the effort you put out is really worth it. Sometimes just talking about a problem makes you feel better. But you'll probably receive sound advice, too. Tell your teacher if you've fallen behind in his or her class or if you don't think you can complete an assignment on time. Perhaps certain adjustments can be made. Find someone to help you plan a schedule that gives you time for yourself, as well as time to get your schoolwork done.

Keep moving. Exercise stimulates the brain and goes a long way toward restoring optimism and reducing anxiety.

Meditate. When you feel anxious or burdened, take some time to center yourself. Breathe slowly and deeply. You might want to quietly repeat affirmations, such as "I am a special person with unique gifts and talents," or "I recognize joy and friendship in my life." Listening to soothing music might also be helpful. Find what works for you.

Eat well. When hunger strikes, reach for natural foods instead of preprocessed snacks. Fresh fruits and vegetables are good for your body and increase your energy. It's also important to eat plenty of protein to keep your brain functioning at high efficiency.

Don't stint on sleep. The old maxim, "Everything looks better in the morning" is only true if you've had enough sleep. When you're exhausted, everything seems overwhelming. But when you're rested, it's easier to muster enthusiasm for the tasks ahead.

Cheating

Everyone knows cheating is wrong. No matter the pressure or workload a person faces, there is always an alternative to cheating. But some studies indicate that cheating is on the rise in middle and high schools. A 2010 study conducted by the Josephson Institute, an organization that researches ethics in society, surveyed forty thousand high school students. Fifty-nine percent acknowledged cheating on a test in the past year. One in three admitted to using the Internet to plagiarize papers.[2] In 2012, a scandal broke in a highly competitive urban high school when seventy-one juniors were caught sharing answers through texting on the state Regents exam. Although such organized, widespread cheating is rare, smaller instances of cheating, such as copying a few math problems or getting advance test information from a friend, occur daily.[3]

"I'm sure everyone understood it was wrong to take other people's work," said a 2010 graduate of the school, "but they had

Some students respond to intense academic pressure by cheating. While you may be able to excuse it as a way to get through a difficult time, cheating is never the right way to succeed.

ways of rationalizing it. Everyone took it as a necessary evil to get through."[4]

Many people disagree vehemently that cheating is a necessary evil. Whatever their rationalizations, most students find it hard to feel good about themselves when they have cheated. And there are practical considerations, too. Academic dishonesty leaves the cheater less prepared to deal with the educational challenges he or she will meet down the road. If a student cheats on a math exam, for instance, he or she will encounter more difficulty with the next semester's math class. If someone hands in an English essay or a history report that is not his or her own, that student is likely to have trouble with future papers he or she is assigned to write. A frequently asked question sums up the dilemma: Would you want to be operated on by a surgeon who cheated in medical school? Cheating robs a student of the chance to develop competence in a given subject or field.

Cheating is also a risky business. If someone is caught cheating, the consequences are unpleasant. A student who might have received a B or a C without cheating may end up with a failing grade on a test or a paper instead. Teachers are getting more skilled at detecting the various ways students may cheat on homework or tests. For example, some students have felt that it's safe to use the Internet to purchase papers. This practice even has a name—cybercheating. But now teachers can submit students' papers to websites that check them against comprehensive databases. The website lets the teacher know if the paper has been taken from the Internet. Many students have been caught this way. There is simply no foolproof way to cheat. The threat of being found out will always add to the academic anxiety that the person doing the cheating already feels.

In many ways, cheating is unfair to the person doing it. It's also unfair to his or her classmates who work hard but receive lower grades. After describing various ways some of her classmates have cheated on tests, a girl in high school explained to writer Denise Clark Pope that cheating "screws over the honest students because the teacher never changes the test and grades everyone on the same curve."[5] This hard-working student refuses to take short cuts herself. Instead she is resolved to "work [her] way to the top the right way, the honest way, by not cheating or cutting class."[6]

Everyone must live with his or her own conscience. Just because other students may be cheating doesn't make it right. Despite pressures and deadlines, the best course of action is simply not to cheat.

Eating Disorders

Grades may be important, but your health is even more important. Intense academic pressure can contribute to an already existing tendency to an eating disorder. Anxiety over grades does not cause the disorder, but tension may make it worse. The main eating disorders that students develop are anorexia, bulimia, and binge eating, also known as compulsive overeating. Although most students who suffer from eating disorders are young women, sometimes boys are also affected. The National Eating Disorders Association has reported that ten million women and girls are struggling with anorexia or bulimia.[7]

The excessive emphasis the media places on body image has contributed to an increased rate of anorexia nervosa. Girls who have anorexia worry about getting fat. They limit their food intake drastically—sometimes literally to the point of starving themselves. Even when they are dangerously underweight, they are afraid to eat. Often they feel cold, weak, and may stop having menstrual periods. Among the more serious symptoms are low blood pressure, heart issues, kidney damage, and osteoporosis, or weaking of the bones.[8] Severe cases may prove fatal.

A number of factors besides body image can increase the likelihood of a person becoming anorexic. These include anxiety, worry, stress, and a desire for perfection. Such characteristics are also associated with academic pressure. Students who feel overwhelmed by their classes or believe they have to be perfect to get into a good

Eating disorders are a result of several different factors, but anxiety is one of them. One thing most anorexics and bulimics share, for example, is the pressure of trying to be perfect.

college may feel their lives are out of control. In a strange, perhaps unconscious, way, they view eating as something that they can control. The sad reality is that once the disease takes over, they have lost control of their eating habits, too. Impaired health may make it difficult for them to concentrate on their studies. They may fall behind in schoolwork, which will increase their academic stress in a vicious circle.

Young women or men with bulimia eat large amounts of food, often when they're not even hungry. This is called bingeing. Although bingeing may provide them a momentary relief from the stress in their lives, academic or otherwise, the relief is short-lived. Afterward, bulimics feel nervous and upset about eating so much. Like anorexics, they worry about gaining weight. So they purge themselves of what they have eaten. Usually, this takes the form of vomiting. Once again, the health risks are alarming. Prolonged periods of bulimia can lead to heart problems and kidney damage, osteoporosis, gum disease, tooth decay, and the eroding of the lining of the esophagus.[9] Death may result from extreme cases of bulimia.

Binge eating is another disorder that affects too many people. For them, eating has become a way to deal with their emotions, such as anger, boredom, or anxiety.[10] Academic pressure may also contribute to the disorder. Hunger has little to do with their eating habits. Eating has become a compulsion.

No one should feel ashamed of having an eating disorder. Anorexia, bulimia, and binge eating are medical conditions for which hope and help are available. Sometimes medicine is prescribed in the first two disorders, but counseling is often the best way to overcome an eating disorder. The patient must understand why his or her eating habits have gotten out of control and learn healthy habits to replace them. It takes a good deal of courage and determination to change. Recovery may be a slow, ongoing process, but it is worth the effort to ensure peace of mind and physical well-being.

Substance Abuse

Sometimes academic pressure in combination with peer pressure leads students to experiment with alcohol or drugs. This is always a mistake. The brief respite one may experience from stress is not worth the significant safety and health risks. Even a small amount of alcohol can result in significant impairment. The danger is that the person doing the drinking may not even realize what is happening.

Substance abuse in the form of using prescription medications for nonmedical reasons poses another danger. Some students have resorted to drugs such as Adderall, a medicine used to treat ADHD, to boost their powers of concentration and alertness. The University

Drinking alcohol or taking drugs may seem like a good way to combat stress, but they actually make things worse.

of Michigan's "Monitoring the Future" study noted an alarming increase in use among high school seniors between 2009 and 2013.[11] Concerned only with their academic performance, students who abuse medications are seldom aware of the possible health consequences. But the unprescribed and medically unsupervised use of Adderall and similar substances may result in fatigue, irritability, headache, nervousness, and loss of appetite. As with the use of illegal drugs, there is also the very real threat of addiction that can take over someone's life.

"The abuse of all prescription medicines is an immediate threat to the health of American teens," according to Steve Pasierb, CEO of Partnership for Drug Free Kids. He classifies the situation as "an epidemic [that] is an entirely preventable adolescent and young adult health crisis."[12]

The best policy is to resist the temptation to drink alcoholic beverages, do drugs, or use prescription medicines for which you have no legitimate use. If you know someone who has fallen prey to one of these scenarios, urge them to get help.

Always Hope

In the worst situations, a teenager may feel so desperate that he or she attempts to harm him- or herself or take their own life. Academic stress may not be the only—or the most important—factor, but it can contribute to feelings of helplessness and despair. A discussion of this issue is beyond the scope of this book. But there is always a way through the most troubling times, and there are always people ready to help and support you. If you have ever felt tempted to harm yourself, tell a parent or guidance counselor at once. The same holds true if a friend confides such feelings to you, even if the friend has asked you not to reveal his or her secret.

What Matters Most

The dangers, both large and small, of intense stress are real. But they can he resisted. Teachers, parents, counselors, and ministers are always ready to help you if the tension becomes too intense. It also helps to remember that grades are not the most important things in the world. Teacher Sarah Mansfield encourages students to gain perspective by asking, "In twenty years, what's going to matter? What am I going to remember?"[13] It's probably not going to be the score on your last chemistry test.

Minds Work in Different Ways

Scientist Carol W. Greider faced some serious challenges during her childhood, including dyslexia. "I had a lot of trouble in school and was put into remedial classes," she told the *New York Times*. "I thought that I was stupid. . . . I had these blinders on that got me through a lot things that might have been obstacles. I just went forward."[1]

The path wasn't easy, but pushing forward, Greider earned a Ph.D. in molecular biology from the University of California at Berkeley, one of the top schools in the nation. In 2009, she won the Nobel Prize for Physiology or Medicine for her study of the role of the enzyme telomerase in protecting chromosomes and preventing aging. Dyslexia did not keep her from a demanding, fulfilling career or making a valuable contribution to the field of biology.

Carol Greider is only one of many gifted persons whose learning styles do not mix well with traditional instruction methods.

Actor Henry Winkler, best known for his iconic role as the Fonz in the 1970's television show *Happy Days,* is another such individual. "I didn't have much support as a student," Winkler recalled on *The Today Show* in 2015. "I was only told that I would never achieve."[2] To empower other youngsters struggling with learning disabilities, Winkler launched a writing career with children's author Lin Oliver. The popular *Here's Hank* book series features a bright young hero who faces many of the same learning challenges Winkler did with energy, imagination, and humor. Some of the books are printed in a special font that dyslexic students find easier to read than regular print.

Because dyslexia and some other learning problems are classified as disorders, many people feel that there is a stigma attached to them. But those with learning disabilities are as bright and capable as anyone else. Their brains simply function differently. Everyone, from the top students to those struggling to get by in their classes, has a unique set of strengths and weaknesses. Instead of labeling students with learning disorders, many psychologists prefer the term learning difference. This eliminates the idea that something is wrong with a student whose learning style doesn't fit easily with those of his or her classmates. "By definition, the term difference has a much less negative connotation than disability," say authors Nancy Boyles and Darlene Contadino in *The Learning Differences Source Book.* "Everybody has the ability to learn, each in his own way."[3]

Whatever way they are characterized, students with learning differences face an uphill battle in the classroom. Sometimes they are not diagnosed for years. An educator may mistake a learning disability for laziness or stubbornness. Sometimes a teacher may even suspect a cognitive impairment. But learning differences are different from cognitive impairment. The latter condition indicates a low potential for intellectual accomplishment. Cognitive impairment places an upper limit on what an individual will be able to accomplish. A learning difference poses no such restrictions. It

Actor Henry Winkler uses his celebrity status to help dyslexic kids learn to enjoy reading. Students with learning disabilities may struggle for years thinking they are not as smart as other kids.

simply requires a student to discover different learning strategies from the ones used in most classrooms.

Types of Learning Differences

The following are among the most common learning disabilities:

Dyslexia—Students with dyslexia have a hard time learning to read. For them, the printed page is like a code they can't decipher. It's estimated that 80 percent of all learning disabilities, or differences, involve reading. About two million children received special help in school to deal with their reading problems in 2003.[4]

Dysgraphia—This learning difference makes it difficult for children to write legibly. They recognize words correctly, but they cannot copy them easily. When they are asked to write a sentence, their words may be jumbled together or take up too much space. Students with dysgraphia have a hard time staying between the lines. Some may have difficulty with spelling and organizing their words on paper.

Dyscalculia—Mathematics pose a great challenge to children with dyscalculia. They find it difficult to do calculations or understand math concepts, such as square roots or simple equations. Once again, this has nothing to do with a child's intelligence. What he or she needs is a different way to handle the material.

Auditory and Visual Processing Differences—Students dealing with these kind of differences see and hear normally. However, they have problems understanding or interpreting what they see or hear. This, of course, makes learning in a traditional classroom setting difficult.

Attention Deficit Disorder (ADD)

Students with ADD do not have problems reading or doing math calculations. They are, however, easily distracted and may find it difficult to concentrate for prolonged periods. Instead of focusing on a single task, they are sensitive to their entire environment. Often they are impulsive, restless, and find it difficult to sit still.

Let's imagine a child named Johnny. The rest of the class may be reading out loud, but Johnny runs to the window to observe a squirrel running up a tree. Then he wanders to the back of the room to examine the books, puzzles, and drawings on the bulletin board. He is interested in almost everything, but he can't sit still. Forced to sit at his desk, Johnny becomes fidgety and jumpy. When a child's activity level becomes excessive in this way, psychologists say that he or she is hyperactive, and he or she is said to have ADHD.

Sometimes it is a child's own thoughts that distract him or her from what's going on. Take the imaginary example of Sandy. The teacher's blue sweater reminds her of the sky, which reminds her

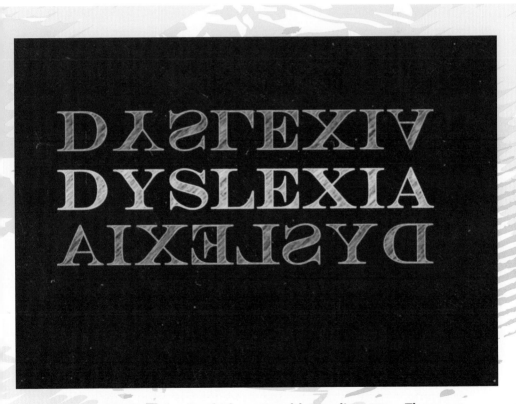

People with dyslexia simply have trouble reading type. There are many different forms and degrees, but this image provides an idea of what a dyslexic might see when reading the center word.

of clouds, which reminds her of flying through the clouds in an airplane, which reminds her of visiting her Aunt Sonja in Florida, which reminds her of seeing crocodiles in the Everglades, and so on. Following her thoughts like a meandering stream, Sandy comes to some interesting places. She is a bright and imaginative child. But she completely misses the teacher's explanation of decimals.

Dealing With Learning Differences

Unfortunately, most schools are not set up to deal with specific needs of students with learning differences. Teachers lack the time to give them individualized instruction. Yet these students with learning differences are expected to master the same material and complete the same assignments as everyone else. They have to meet the same requirements for promotion into the next grade or for graduation from high school. Although the situation sounds discouraging, a student with a learning difference can sometimes work out special accommodations with the school that take his or her unique learning style into consideration.

In order to qualify, the student has to be officially diagnosed by an educational specialist. This may involve answering questions and completing tests designed to reveal a student's strengths and weaknesses. Once the diagnosis is made, parents, teachers, and perhaps an educational psychologist develop a plan. This is called an Individualized Education Plan, or IEP. Specific differences are taken into consideration and strategies worked out to help the child succeed. For example, children with learning differences often tire more quickly than their classmates. This leaves them with less energy to do their homework. What the teacher meant as a short assignment might take them hours. Under these circumstances, special accommodations might be made for homework. Perhaps the student receives shorter assignments or is given time to work at school. Other accommodations might include more time to complete tests, special periods with a tutor, frequent access to a computer, help with organization, or even someone to read test questions with them. It all depends on the individual student's needs.

Mastering Challenges

Claudia Porter, founder of The Porter Academy in Roswell, Georgia, also believes in individualized instruction. The students who attend her private grade school have suffered a great deal of disappointment and frustration in school. "You need to work with the whole child to make her feel good about herself," Porter emphasizes.[5] Believing that a pressure-free environment allows children to grow and learn most easily, Porter does not give grades. But teachers do assign homework. Exercise, occupational therapy, art, music, and drama are integrated into a curriculum that also focuses on the basics of reading, writing, and arithmetic. "I don't take behavior problems," explains Porter, "but I do take frustrated kids who are striking out because they don't know what else to do."[6] Porter and her staff teach them how to meet and master their unique challenges.

Learning How You Learn

Everyone has his or her own learning style. Sometimes that style fits in well with a classroom routine. Sometimes it does not. Every student must discover what suits him or her best. But just because a student learns differently from his or her classmates does not make him or her any less intelligent. People with learning differences have found success in every field from acting to science to sports. For example, dysgraphia didn't prevent mystery writer Agatha Christie from becoming the "queen of the who-done-it's." Steven Spielberg, not diagnosed with dyslexia until he was an adult, used filmmaking as a way to deal with his learning difference. And former football quarterback Tim Tebow, who learned of his dyslexia at age seven, found that he learns best when he moves around rather than sitting still, a technique known as kinesthetic learning.

"There's a lot of people that have certain processing disabilities, and it has nothing to do with your intelligence," says Tebow, who

Some students respond best to receiving academic help from another student. A peer tutor might be able to explain things in ways a teacher might not think of.

hopes that his experiences will encourage others with learning differences to take heart. His message to them is simple: "Hey, this isn't something that's a handicap. You just have to learn how you learn and overcome it. It's something you can be better off because of, because you know you learn."[7] The key to Tebow's success and to children facing similar challenges is hard work, determination, and caring adults to help smooth the way.

Tips to Beat Stress

At Lexington High School in Massachusetts, students danced in the halls as loud speakers filled the air with music. They kept straight faces (or tried to) when their teachers showed up in class wearing big red clown noses. Outdoors, they blew bubbles and decorated the pavement with sidewalk chalk. Yoga classes and mindfulness training rounded out the school's second Stress Reduction Day in May of 2013. "Kids just got to be kids and play," said wellness teacher Julie Fenn. "It's been fun to see even our big boys blowing bubbles and laughing."[1] Administrators at Lexington have worked hard to lessen stress among a highly competitive student body. Although stress levels had fallen since 2004, a survey conducted in 2011 found 40 percent of the participants had "a lot of stress" while 11 percent reported "extreme stress."[2] To help alleviate the problem, Lexington stopped publishing the honor roll in the local paper and stopped appointing a valedictorian and salutatorian to speak at graduation.

"Everyone has extreme goals and they want to do really well, and stress is a part of that," said Senior Class President Zach Strohmeyer in 2013. "It's just important that we recognize that it's there and have ways to deal with it."[3]

Mindfulness Training

Some schools have turned to a practice called mindfulness training to help students handle pressure. Students are taught to relax and take deep breaths while they concentrate on the present moment, their surroundings, and their feelings. It sounds simple—and it is simple—but many students have successfully used the technique to cope with academic and social anxieties and other negative emotions. A year-long class offered at Wilson High School in Portland, Oregon, has students practicing a variety of ways to focus on the present, including yoga, meditation, deep breathing, visualization, keeping a journal, and listening without passing judgment. "This class helps me bring more attention to my breath and overcome [panic attacks]," reported one student. "I'm less stressed out and better able to cope with stress."[4]

Actress Goldie Hawn believes strongly in the benefits of mindfulness training. Working closely with education specialists, psychologists, and neuroscientists, she started a program named MindUp to introduce children to the practice. "A stressed brain and a brain that doesn't feel good is basically a brain that doesn't focus or learn as well," Hawn explained.[5] In one MindUp exercise, students learn to concentrate on their breathing for two to three minutes, thereby giving themselves a brain break. Worries and fears fade away in the peaceful rhythm of inhale, exhale, inhale, exhale. Hawn's foundation reports that between 2011 and 2015, about 13,500 teachers and 405,000 students in the United States have tried MindUp.[6] Schools in Canada and the United Kingdom have also used the program.

Even if your school offers no class in mindfulness training, you can adopt the practice on your own. Therapist Barbara Ter Haar adds

Meditation can help combat stress and anxiety. Studies show that various relaxation techniques—even deep breathing—can reduce stress and improve concentration.

that self-expression can be an important part of the process and an effective way to sort through your feelings. You can experiment with different mediums, such as poetry, art, singing, dancing, talking, or anything else you'd like to try. In drawing or painting, you can use colors to reveal your feelings—perhaps red for anxiety and green for hope. Or mix that around. The colors can mean anything you want. As Ter Haar notes, "There's no right or wrong way to draw."[7] Losing yourself for a time in a simple act of creation or even just venting to a parent or friend can help dispel negativity and add balance to your life.

Practical Tips

Relaxation techniques and brain breaks can offer valuable help in dealing with stress. Another way to reduce anxieties is to work efficiently so you don't get behind or let assignments pile up. To keep on top of your work and minimize stress, it helps to do a quick review of what goes on in your classes each day. By reviewing your history or science notes—even when it's not assigned—you allow the material to sink more deeply into your mind. You can think of this as the mental equivalent of highlighting text on a page. Regular reviews will help you learn material more quickly and efficiently.

And that's what we're going to do to conclude this chapter: review. Some of the do's and don'ts listed below have already been mentioned in this book, but they're important enough to go over one more time. They can help you do well in school and beat stress at the same time.

Do take care of yourself first. Eat wisely, and get enough sleep. Exhaustion can make everything seem worse. You don't want to take a test tired or hungry.

Do keep moving. A sign advertising a fitness club announces, "Stressed is desserts spelled backwards. Work off both." This is excellent advice. Psychologists say that exercise is one of the greatest of all stress-busters.

Do carve your own space. This can be a room or part of one, a corner of the porch, or a desk or table with a comfortable chair. This is your stress-free zone where you can relax, listen to music, read for pleasure, or simply think.

Do be imaginative. It isn't always easy to be creative when extracurricular activities engage you after school or when homework piles up. But it pays to carve out a little time, maybe ten or fifteen minutes, for something you enjoy. It might be sketching, playing the guitar, or cooking—whatever you find relaxing and fun.

Do ask for help. If you're feeling worried because you don't understand a class or fear you can't keep up with the workload, tell someone. Parents, teachers, and counselors want what's best for you emotionally, as well as academically. They may suggest tutoring or changing the level of your class. They may have study tips to offer. And they can reassure you that you're not alone in your academic challenges.

Do keep track of your assignments. A little organization goes a long way. Maintain a regular study schedule. Write down when assignments are due, and plan how much time you need to complete them. Prioritize what needs to be done. Don't wait until the last minute to study for a test or begin a project.

Do take a break when you find it hard to focus. Sometimes it helps to time yourself. Concentrate for half an hour, or whatever time works for you, then give yourself a ten minute break.

Don't forget your friends are in the same boat. Studying with friends can be helpful as long as you focus on the material to be covered. Quizzing each other is an excellent way to review for a test. A friend may be able to help you understand an algebra problem or a theory you didn't quite grasp in history. When it's your turn to explain to someone else, you'll be reinforcing your own knowledge, too. And if you can't get together in person, counselor Gayle Hamilton recommends you reach for your phone.[8]

Don't fill up every waking moment. No one can do everything. Limit your after-school involvements. Do not feel you have to take part in everything to look good on your college application. Leadership teacher Sarah Mansfield advises students to be enthusiastic about what they do. "Find your passion. Give 110 percent to what you love." It might be scouting, church activities, music, or athletics. But, she cautions, "Don't sign up for everything."[9]

Don't make grades too important. Of course, you want to work for good grades. But your whole future does not depend on your grades, your test scores, or where you go to college. Determination and enthusiasm count for more.

Don't keep your feelings bottled inside. When the workload becomes burdensome, talk to you parents or school counselor.

Physical exercise, spending time with friends, and laughter are all helpful ways to reduce feelings of stress. While success in school is important, personal relationships and your health are, too.

Don't compare yourself to others. Aim to do the best work you can do—not to beat your classmates. What you learn is more important than where you rank in the class.

Do find something to laugh about, whether you are relaxing with friends, watching a funny television show, or playing with your pet. The old saying, "Laugher is the best medicine" has a good deal of truth behind it. Laughter reduces stress hormones and decreases anxiety. It can also boost your energy level, which enables you to work more efficiently.

Do something nice for someone. It doesn't have to big or time-consuming. You might stop to chat with an elderly neighbor, read a picture book to a younger sibling, or reach out to a classmate who seems lonely. Simple, quiet gestures can make a big difference to others. They also let you feel good about yourself, and that's a huge stress-buster.

Challenges and Opportunities

Students in the early twenty-first century face more challenges and pressure than at any other time in the history of American education. They also enjoy unprecedented opportunities. But no student should be so goal oriented or worried about good grades and college that he or she ceases to enjoy each day. "Don't be disturbed by past failure or fear of future failure," advises Barbara Ter Haar.[10] There's a lot to be said for living in the moment—working hard but taking time for fun. Making the most of your school years does not mean doing perfect assignments and getting perfect test scores. Growing into a happy, confident individual and a life-long learner is what matters most.

Chapter Notes

Chapter 1: An A for Everyone?

1. Helen Wright, *Sweeper in the Sky: The Life of Maria Mitchell, First Woman Astronomer in America* (New York, N.Y.: The Macmillan Company, 1949).
2. David Elkind, *The Hurried Child: Growing Up Too Fast Too Soon* (Reading, Mass.: Addison-Wesley Publishing Company, 1981), p. 48.
3. William Crain, *Reclaiming Childhood: Letting Children Be Children in Our Achievement-Oriented Society* (New York, N.Y.: Henry Holt and Company, 2003), p. 151.

Chapter 2: Grade School and Middle School: "So Little Time to Be Kids"

1. Email from Elizabeth McGhee, March 7, 2015.
2. Serena Gersten, "Kindergarten Has Become Too Stressful With Unrealistic Expectations," *New York Times*, May 29, 2012, <http://www.newstimes.com/opinion/article/Sarina-Gersten-Kindergarten-has-become-too-3593119.php>.
3. Ibid.
4. Pam Hartigan, "Pressure-Cooker Kindergarten," *Boston.com*, August 30, 2009, <http://www.boston.com/yourtown/waltham/articles/2009/08/30/pressure_cooker_kindergarten/>.
5. Telephone interview with Maria Edmunds, February 9, 2015.
6. Ibid.
7. Dayna Straehley, "Lake Elsinore: Students Learn Lessons—By Playing," *Press Enterprise*, February 3, 2015, <http://www.pe.com/articles/play-759603-students-school.html>.
8. Telephone interview with Tim Bedley, February 23, 2015.

9. Eric Pace, "William A. Alexander, 84, Dies; Fostered Idea of Middle Schools," *New York Times*, August 29, 1996, <http://www.nytimes.com/1996/08/29/us/william-m-alexander-84-dies-fostered-idea-of-middle-schools.html>.

10. Telephone interview with Gayle Hamilton, February 2015.

11. Ibid.

12. Laura Pappano, "Is Your First Grader College Ready?" *New York Times*, February 4, 2014, <http://www.nytimes.com/2015/02/08/education/edlife/is-your-first-grader-college-ready.html?_r=0>.

13. Ibid.

14. Ibid.

Chapter 3: High School: Menu of Options

1. Personal interview with Lana Krumweide, February 23, 2015.

2. Ibid.

3. Alexandra Pannoni, "Discover the Difference Between AP and IB Classes," *U.S. News and World Report*, September 2, 2014, <http://www.usnews.com/education/blogs/high-school-notes/2014/09/02/discover-the-difference-between-ap-and-ib-classes>.

4. Ibid.

5. Devon Haynie, "Decide If a STEM High School Is Right for Your Child," *U.S. News and World Report*, April 23, 2014, <http://www.usnews.com/education/best-high-schools/articles/2014/04/23/decide-if-a-stem-high-school-is-right-for-your-child>.

6. Ibid.

7. Interview with Bryan Carr, October 10, 2007.

8. Jason Koebler, "International Baccalaureate Creates 4000th Program Worldwide," *U.S. News and World Report*, July 5, 2011, <http://www.usnews.com/education/blogs/high-school-notes/2011/07/05/international-baccalaureate-creates-

4000th-program-worldwide>.

9. Interview with Paul Fleisher, April 4, 2007.

10. Alexandra Robbins, *The Overachievers: The Secret Lives of Driven Kids* (New York, N.Y.: Hyperion, 2006), p. 50.

11. Alexandra Pannoni, "3 Answers for High School Parents About AVID Classes," *U.S. News and World Report,* February 9, 2015, <http://www.usnews.com/education/blogs/high-school-notes/2015/02/09/3-answers-for-high-school-parents-about-avid-classes>.

12. Interview with Jennifer Coleman, October 10, 2007.

Chapter 4: Homework: Then and Now

1. Gracie Bonds Staples, "Beware of Backpacks: 14,000 Children Treated Yearly for Injuries," *Atlanta Journal Constitution,* September 9, 2013, <http://www.jsonline.com/news/health/beware-of-backpacks-14000-children-treated-yearly-for-injuries-b9984635z1-222888831.html>.

2. Bruce Feiler, "The Homework Squabbles," *New York Times,* September 12, 2014, <http://www.nytimes.com/2014/09/14/fashion/the-homework-squabbles.html?_r=0>.

3. Valerie Strauss, "Life Support: A History of Homework," *Pittsburgh Post-Gazette.com,* November 6, 2003, <http://old.post-gazette.com/lifestyle/20031106life6.asp>.

4. Brian P. Gill and Steven L. Schlossman, "Villain or Savior? The American Discourse on Homework, 1850–2003," *Theory Into Practice,* vol. 43, no. 3, 2004, College of Education, The Ohio State University, p. 175.

5. Bonds.

6. Ibid.

7. "History of Homework," *SFGate.com,* December 19, 1999, <http://www.sfgate.com/news/article/HISTORY-OF-HOMEWORK-3053660.php>.

8. Archived Information, *A Nation at Risk*, April 1983, <https://www2.ed.gov/pubs/NatAtRisk/risk.html>.

9. Alfie Kohn, *The Homework Myth: Why Our Kids Get Too Much of a Good Thing* (Cambridge, Mass.: Da Capo Press, 2006), p. 120.

10. Ibid.

Chapter 5: Taming the Homework Monster

1. KJ Dell'Antonia, "Homework's Emotional Toll on Students and Families," *New York Times*, March 1, 2014, <http://parenting.blogs.nytimes.com/2014/03/12/homeworks-emotional-toll-on-students-and-families/?_r=0>.

2. Ibid.

3. Interview with Jeffrey Doyle, October 10, 2007.

4. "ZZZ's to A Act Aims to Keep Kids Awake in Class," *wsoctv.com*, September 2, 2014, <http://www.wsoctv.com/news/news/zzzs-s-act-aims-keep-kids-awake-class/nhR3y/>.

5. "Let Them Sleep: AAP Recommends Delaying Start Times of Middle and High Schools to Combat Teen Sleep Deprivation," *American Academy of Pediatrics*, August 25, 2014, <https://www.aap.org/en-us/about-the-aap/aap-press-room/Pages/Let-Them-Sleep-AAP-Recommends-Delaying-Start-Times-of-Middle-and-High-Schools-to-Combat-Teen-Sleep-Deprivation.aspx>.

6. Ibid.

7. Alfie Kohn, *The Schools Our Children Deserve: Moving Beyond Traditional Classrooms and Tougher Standards* (Boston, Mass.: Houghton Mifflin Company, 1999), p. 28.

8. Denise Clark Pope, *"Doing School": How We are Creating a Generation of Stressed Out, Materialistic, and Miseducated Students* (New Haven, Conn.: Yale University Press, 2001), p. 60.

9. Personal interview with student, September 4, 2007.

Chapter 6: High Stakes Tests and How They Got Started

1. "'Listen: The Movie' Challenges the Culture of Standardized Testing," *Edutopia*, October 15, 2013, <http://www.edutopia.org/blog/listen-movie-challenges-standardized-testing-todd-finley>.

2. Ibid.

3. Linda Perlstein, *Tested: One American School Struggles to Make the Grade* (New York, N.Y.: Henry Holt and Company, 2007), p. 29.

4. Ibid., p.32.

5. Jared T. Bigham, EdD, *The Common Core Standards*, Idiot's Guides series (New York, N.Y.: Penguin Group (USA) Inc., 2015), pp. 7-8.

6. Stacy Teicher Khadaroo, "No Child Left Behind 101: Where Lawmakers Agree, Disagree," *Christian Science Monitor*, February 25, 2015, <http://www.csmonitor.com/USA/2015/0225/No-Child-Left-Behind-101-where-lawmakers-agree-disagree>.

7. Elizabeth Harris, "As Common Core Testing Is Ushered In, Parents and Students Opt Out," *New York Times*, March 1, 2015, <http://www.nytimes.com/2015/03/02/nyregion/as-common-core-testing-is-ushered-in-parents-and-students-opt-out.html?_r=0>.

8. Perlstein, p. 120.

9. Ibid., p. 123.

10. David Elkind, *The Hurried Child: Growing Up Too Fast Too Soon* (Reading, Mass.: Addison-Wesley Publishing Company, 1981), p. 25.

11. Interview with Lana Krumweide, February 23, 2015.

12. Lisa Chipongian, "What is 'Brain-Based Learning?" *Brain Connection*, March 26, 2004, <http://brainconnection.brainhq.com/2004/03/26/what-is-brain-based-learning/>.

Chapter 7: Getting Into College

1. Jeremy Anderberg, "Is College for Everyone? An Introduction and Timeline of College in America," *The Art of Manliness*, March 5, 2014, <http://www.artofmanliness.com/2014/03/05/is-college-for-everyone-an-introduction-and-timeline-of-college-in-america/>.

2. Ibid.

3. "The College Dropouts Hall of Fame: Rich, Famous, and Successful People Who Were High School or College Dropouts," <http://www.collegedropoutshalloffame.com/g.htm>.

4. Alexandra Robbins, *The Overachievers: The Secret Lives of Driven Kids* (New York, N.Y.: Hyperion, 2006), p. 300.

5. Justin Peligri, "No, the SAT Is Not Required. More Colleges Join Test-Optional Train," *USA Today*, July 7, 2014, <http://college.usatoday.com/2014/07/07/no-the-sat-is-not-required-more-colleges-join-test-optional-train/>.

6. Ibid.

7. Ibid.

8. Lauren Gensler, "10 Things You Need To Know To Successfully Navigate the Common App," *Forbes*, November 17, 2014, <http://www.forbes.com/sites/laurengensler/2014/11/17/10-things-you-need-to-know-to-successfully-navigate-the-common-app-2/>.

9. Ibid.

10. Ben Tracy, "UCLA: Kids Today More Stressed Out, Partying Less Than Their Parents Did," *CBS News*, February 5, 2014, <http://www.cbsnews.com/news/parents-partied-harder-than-todays-high-schoolers-says-ucla/>.

11. Ibid.

12. Marion Sammartino, "School Days: Spring Doldrums and College Admissions," *North County Times*, March 30, 1999.

13. Interview with Bryan Carr, October 10, 2007.

14. PageSix.com staff, "Look Who Harvard Blew Off," May 22, 2007, <http://pagesix.com/2007/05/22/look-who-harvard-blew-off/>.

15. Telephone interview with Mickey VanDerwerker, July 25, 2005.

Chapter 8: When Stress Becomes Overwhelming

1. Interview with Autumn Nabors, October 10, 2007.

2. Vivian Yee, "Stuyvesant Students Describe the How and Why of Cheating," *New York Times,* September 25, 2012, <http://www.nytimes.com/2012/09/26/education/stuyvesant-high-school-students-describe-rationale-for-cheating.html?_r=0>.

3. Ibid."

4. Ibid.

5. Denise Clark Pope, *"Doing School": How We are Creating a Generation of Stressed Out, Materialistic, and Miseducated Students* (New Haven, Conn.: Yale University Press, 2001), p 40.

6. Ibid., p. 40.

7. "Anorexia Nervosa—Topic Overview," *WebMD,* n.d. <http://www.webmd.com/mental-health/eating-disorders/anorexia-nervosa/anorexia-nervosa-topic-overview>.

8. Ibid.

9. "Bulimia Nervosa—Topic Overview," *WebMD,* n.d. <http://www.webmd.com/mental-health/eating-disorders/bulimia-nervosa/bulimia-nervosa-topic-overview>.

10. "Binge Eating Disorder," *Athealth.com,* modified June 2008, <http://athealth.com/topics/binge-eating-disorder/>.

11. Josie Feliz, "Adderall Abuse Increases Among High School Students," *Partnership for Drug-Free Kids,* December 18, 2013, <http://www.drugfree.org/newsroom/adderall-abuse-increases-among-high-school-students/>.

12. Ibid.

13. Interview with Sarah Mansfield, October 10, 2007.

Chapter 9: Minds Work in Different Ways

1. Claudia Dreifus, "A Conversation With Carol Greider: On Winning a Nobel Prize in Science, *New York Times*, October 13, 2009, <http://www.nytimes.com/2009/10/13/science/13conv.html>.

2. Jessica Mazzola, "Henry Winkler Shares His Latest Book With N.J. Kids," *NJ.com*, February 10, 2015, <http://www.nj.com/essex/index.ssf/2015/02/henry_winkler_shares_latest_book_with_nj_kids.html>.

3. Nancy S. Boyles, M.Ed. and Darlene Contadino, M.S.W., *The Learning Differences Sourcebook* (Los Angeles, Calif.: Lowell House, 1997), pp. 16–17.

4. Sally Shaywitz, *Overcoming Dyslexia: A New and Complete Science-Based Program for Reading Problems at Any Level* (New York, N.Y.: Alfred A. Knopf, 2003), p. 29.

5. Telephone interview with Claudia Porter, October 9, 2007.

6. Ibid.

7. Brian Costello, "Dyslexia Could Never Sack Jets' Tebow, *New York Post*, August 3, 2012, <http://nypost.com/2012/08/03/dyslexia-could-never-sack-jets-tebow/>.

Chapter 10: Tips to Beat Stress

1. Kathleen Burge, "Lexington Tries to Tackle High School Student Stress," *Boston Globe*, May 30, 2013, <http://www.bostonglobe.com/metro/regionals/west/2013/05/29/lexington-tries-tackle-high-school-student-stress/6lSLFCZ9tIcnSY1bhfYylN/story.html>.

2. Ibid.

3. Ibid.

4. Gloria Wozniacka, "Mindfulness Training Helps Teens cope With Stress and Anxiety," *Washington Post*, December 15, 2014, <http://www.washingtonpost.com/national/

health-science/mindfulness-training-helps-teens-cope-with-stress-and-anxiety/2014/12/12/589574fe-7bf6-11e4-b821-503cc7efed9e_story.html>.

5. Emily Holland, "Can 'Mindfulness' Help Students Do Better in School?" *Wall Street Journal*, February 16, 2015, <http://www.wsj.com/articles/can-mindfulness-help-students-do-better-in-school-1424145647>.

6. Ibid.

7. Interview with Barbara Ter Haar, February 2015.

8. Interview with Gayle Hamilton, October 10, 2007.

9. Interview with Sarah Mansfield, October 10, 2007.

10. Interview with Barbara Ter Haar, February 2015.

Glossary

adequate yearly progress (AYP)—A way to evaluate a school's effectiveness based on the annual improvement in students' standardized test scores. A minimum AYP is required by the No Child Left Behind Act.

Advanced Placement classes—College-level classes taught in high school.

anorexia—An eating disorder, primarily affecting young women, in which a person eats so little that he or she becomes emaciated.

attention deficit disorder (ADD)—A learning disability or difference that is characterized by impulsivity and distractibility.

auditory processing difference—A learning disability or difference that affects the way students learn spoken material.

AVID (Advancement Via Individual Determination)—A program to help high school students with potential prepare for college.

binge eating—Compulsive overeating.

bulimia—An eating disorder, primarily affecting young women, in which a person eats large amounts of food and then purges him- or herself.

charter schools—Publicly funded elementary and high schools that are run independently of local school districts.

circadian rhythm—A biological cycle that determines a person's optimum sleep/wake schedule.

cognitive impairment—A condition that limits what an individual may learn or accomplish.

Common Core—A set of academic standards in math and English that has been adopted in most states.

cybercheating—A risky practice of buying papers over the Internet.

depression—A psychiatric condition that may be characterized by feelings of sadness, lack of energy, and an inability to concentrate, as well as other symptoms.

dyscalculia—A learning disability or difference that affects the way a student learns mathematics.

dysgraphia—A learning disability or difference that affects a student's handwriting.

dyslexia—A learning disability or difference that affects the way a student learns to read.

early decision—An option in which applicants to a particular college may be accepted several months before the main body of students.

grade point average (GPA)—Overall average of all the grades a student has taken in which an A counts for 4 points, B for 3, C for 2, D for 1. In AP classes an extra point is added.

individualized education plan (IEP)—A set of special accommodations tailored to meet the specific needs of students with learning disabilities or differences.

International Baccalaureate—An international educational program that emphasizes global issues and offers college credits in high school.

learning disability—One of several conditions in which a student may process information differently from the way the majority of his or her classmates do. Children with learning disabilities or differences may require special techniques to master educational skills.

magnet schools—High-performance schools with a particular emphasis, such as science and math or the performing arts.

mindfulness training—A practice that combines breath control and meditation to increase awareness of the moment and sharpen concentration.

No Child Left Behind Act—Federal legislation that mandates standardized tests at designated grades and imposes penalties on schools with low test scores.

Preliminary Scholastic Aptitude Test (PSAT)—A test taken by college-bound students in preparation for the Scholastic Aptitude Test (SAT).

progressive movement—An educational philosophy, popular in the 1930s, that looked beyond academics to focus on the physical and emotional needs of students.

SAT Reasoning Test (formerly known as the Scholastic Aptitude Test or the Scholastic Achievement Test)—A test taken by college-bound students to gauge their potential for verbal and mathematical learning.

SAT Subject Tests (formerly known as achievement tests or SAT IIs)—College entrance exams that test a student's aptitude in a particular subject, such as geometry or French.

STEM schools—High-performance science, technology, engineering, and math high schools.

student burnout—A condition whereby students lose motivation and interest in their studies.

test anxiety—A condition in which students become overly fearful of taking tests.

test-optional schools—Colleges that do not require applicants to submit test scores from college boards, such as the SAT.

visual processing difference—A learning disability or difference that affects the way a student perceives written material.

For More Information

American Academy of Child and Adolescent Psychiatry

P.O. Box 96106

Washington, DC 20090

aacap.org

Association for Mindfulness in Education

mindfuleducation.org

The Hawn Foundation: MindUp

thehawnfoundation.org/mindup

Learning Disabilities Association of America

4156 Library Road

Pittsburgh, PA 15234-1349

(412) 341-1515

ldaamerica.org

National Association of School Psychologists

4340 East West Highway, Suite 402

Bethesda, MD 20814

(301) 657-0270

nasponline.org

National Center for Learning Disabilities

32 Laight Street, Second Floor

New York, NY 10013

ncld.org

National Education Association (NEA)

1201 16th St. NW

Washington, DC 20036-3290

(202) 833-4000

nea.org

US Department of Agriculture Food and Nutrition Information Center

fnic.nal.usda.gov/about-fnic

Web Sites

pamf.org/teen/life/stress/academicpressure.html

The Sutter Health Palo Alto Medical Foundation discusses the different sources of academic pressure.

pbskids.org/itsmylife/school/highschool/article5.html

PBS Kids offers tips on how to succeed in high school.

educationcorner.com/study-skills.html

Education Corner discusses study skills for students.

Further Reading

Biegel, Gina, *The Stress Reduction Workbook For Teens: Mindfulness Skills to Help You Deal With Stress*. Oakland, Calif.: New Harbinger Publications, 2010.

Dolin, Ann K. *Homework Made Simple: Tips, Tools, and Solutions to Stress-Free Homework*. Washington, D.C.: Advantage Books, 2010.

Hipp, Earl. *Fighting Invisible Tigers: Stress Management for Teens*. Minneapolis, Minn.: Free Spirit Publishing, 2008.

Moss, Wendy, PhD and Robin DeLuca-Acconi, LCSW. *School Made Easier: A Kid's Guide to Study Strategies and Anxiety-Busting Tools*. Washington, D.C.: Magination Press, American Psychological Association, 2013.

Willard, Christopher, PsyD. *Mindfulness for Teen Anxiety: A Workbook for Overcoming Anxiety at Home, at School, and Everywhere Else*. Oakland, Calif.: New Harbinger Publications, 2014.

Index

in quality assessment, 10, 44, 57

reform of, 54

as stressor, 8, 51, 57–58

student preparation, 31

teachers and, 8, 10, 31, 55, 57

STEM schools, 26

Stibor, Ryann, 69

stress

academic pressure as, 23, 31, 57, 78, 83, 85–86

burnout, 78–79

coping skills, 100

sleep deprivation, 40–41, 43–44, 46, 80, 102

stress reduction day, 99

student's responses to, 14, 29, 44, 59, 69, 78, 85–86, 100

tolerance for, 78

stretch schools, 72, 74

Strohmeyer, Zach, 100

study tips, 44, 103

substance abuse, 78, 86

T

teachers

standardized tests and, 8, 10, 31, 55, 57

system demands on, 8, 10, 14, 16, 57, 82, 94

teaching to the test, 16, 55, 57

Tebow, Tim, 95, 97

Ter Haar, Barbara, 100, 102, 105

test anxiety, 47–49, 57

test-optional schools, 66

V

VanDerwerker, Mickey, 75

Vieira, Meredith, 75

W

Walker, Francis, 34

Wilson High School, 100

Winkler, Henry, 90

Z

Zuckerberg, Mark, 61

ZZZ's to A Act, 43